# PRACTICAL HELPS *for a* HURTING CHURCH

## A STUDY OF 1 CORINTHIANS 6:12–11:34

## BIBLE STUDY GUIDE

From the Bible-teaching ministry of

*Charles R. Swindoll*

INSIGHT FOR LIVING

Charles R. Swindoll is a graduate of Dallas Theological Seminary and has served in pastorates for more than twenty-four years, including churches in Texas, New England, and California. Since 1971 he has served as senior pastor of the First Evangelical Free Church of Fullerton, California. Chuck's radio program, "Insight for Living," began in 1979. In addition to his church and radio ministries, Chuck has written twenty-three books and numerous booklets on a variety of subjects.

This guide is the second in a three-part series on the book of 1 Corinthians. Based on the outlines of Chuck's sermons, the study guide text is coauthored by Julie Martin, a graduate of Biola University. The Living Insights are written by Bill Butterworth, a graduate of Florida Bible College, Dallas Theological Seminary, and Florida Atlantic University. Julie Martin is an associate editor in the Educational Products Department at Insight for Living, and Bill Butterworth is currently a staff writer in the Educational Products Department.

| | |
|---|---|
| **Editor in Chief:** | Cynthia Swindoll |
| **Coauthor of Text:** | Julie Martin |
| **Author of Living Insights:** | Bill Butterworth |
| **Copy Manager:** | Jac La Tour |
| **Senior Copy Editor:** | Jane Gillis |
| **Copy Editor:** | Wendy Peterson |
| **Director, Communications Division:** | Carla Beck |
| **Project Manager:** | Nina Paris |
| **Project Supervisor:** | Cassandra Clark |
| **Art Director:** | Donna Mayo |
| **Production Artists:** | Wanda Roberts and Diana Vasquez |
| **Typographer:** | Bob Haskins |
| **Cover Photographer:** | Lynne Scanlon/Comstock Inc. |
| **Print Production Manager:** | Deedee Snyder |
| **Printer:** | Frye and Smith |

# Ordering Information

An album that contains twelve messages on six cassettes and corresponds to this study guide may be purchased through the Sales Department of Insight for Living, Post Office Box 4444, Fullerton, California 92634. For ordering information and a current catalog, please write our office or call (714) 870-9161.

Canadian residents may obtain a catalog and ordering information through Insight for Living Ministries, Post Office Box 2510, Vancouver, British Columbia, Canada V6B 3W7, (604) 272-5811. Australian residents should direct their correspondence to Insight for Living Ministries, General Post Office Box 2823 EE, Melbourne, Victoria 3001. Other overseas residents should direct their correspondence to our Fullerton office.

If you wish to order by Visa or MasterCard, you are welcome to use our toll-free number, (800) 772-8888, Monday through Friday, between the hours of 8:30 A.M. and 4:00 P.M., Pacific time. This number may be used anywhere in the United States except Alaska, California, and Hawaii. Orders from these areas can be made by calling our general office number, (714) 870-9161. Orders from Canada can be made by calling (604) 272-5811.

# Table of Contents

# Practical Helps for a Hurting Church
## A Study of 1 Corinthians 6:12–11:34

*The central section of 1 Corinthians focuses our thoughts on some extremely controversial issues. Because of the nature of each one, we need to pay close attention to what God says rather than what human tradition or opinion says. How greatly we need to hear the Word of the Lord!*

*As you will soon discover, these chapters address practical problems . . . crucial questions, like:*

> *How should I handle my sexual desires?*
> *Is it OK to remain single?*
> *How can I handle an unhappy marriage?*
> *Are there taboos we should shun?*
> *Should hats be worn by women in worship?*
> *Does observance of the Lord's Table have certain*
>     *requirements?*

*Paul, under the inspiration of the Holy Spirit, writes specific principles for our personal use. What spoke to God's people then still speaks to God's people today. We want to be sure that it is* His *truth we are hearing . . . not a misinterpretation of such.*

*Please do pray as you hear and then heed what God has preserved in this crucial section of His Book.*

*Chuck Swindoll*

# Putting Truth into Action

Knowledge apart from application falls short of God's desire for His children. Knowledge must result in change and growth. Consequently, we have constructed this Bible study guide with these purposes in mind: (1) to stimulate discovery, (2) to increase understanding, and (3) to encourage application.

At the end of each lesson is a section called 🖼️ *Living Insights.* There you'll be given assistance in further Bible study, and you'll be encouraged to contemplate and apply the things you've learned. This is the place where the lesson is fitted with shoe leather for your walk through the varied experiences of life.

It's our hope that you'll discover numerous ways to use this tool. Some useful avenues we suggest are personal meditation, joint discovery, and discussion with your spouse, family, work associates, friends, or neighbors. The study guide is also practical for Sunday school classes, Bible study groups, and, of course, as a study aid for the "Insight for Living" radio broadcast.

In order to derive the greatest benefit from this process, we suggest that you record your responses to the lessons in the space which has been provided for you. In view of the kinds of questions asked, your study guide may become a journal filled with your many discoveries and commitments. We anticipate that you will find yourself returning to it periodically for review and encouragement.

*Julie Martin*
*Coauthor of Text*

*Bill Butterworth*
*Author of Living Insights*

# PRACTICAL HELPS *for a* HURTING CHURCH

## A STUDY OF 1 CORINTHIANS 6:12–11:34

# My Body and Me

*1 Corinthians 6:12-20*

We live in an age infatuated with the human body. Each year billions of dollars are spent on cosmetics, exercise equipment, fitness clubs, fashion, vitamins, and diet books. Beautiful, finely tuned bodies are paraded before us in every form of media. The perfect body, we're told, is the one with the sleekest form and firmest muscles.

Along with the body craze has come an obsession with sex that has reached insane proportions. The media promotes it for all it's worth, constantly exploiting our God-given sexual desires.

Nothing new—this obsession. We find that the same issues surfaced in ancient Corinth more than nineteen hundred years ago.

The Corinthian Christians had perverted God's view of the human body. Imbalanced in yet another area, they had fallen off the spiritual tightrope and landed headfirst on the hard, cold, cement consequences of sin. In 1 Corinthians 6:12-20, Paul not only picks them up and sets them back on their feet but brings balance to our contemporary extremism as well.

## I. Background on the Body

Although many modern beliefs are reflected in the Corinthians' behavior, their view of the human body differed greatly from ours. They believed, like other Greeks and Romans, that the body was the prison or tomb of the soul. They thought the body itself had no moral value, but because of its sensual appetites, it seduced the soul to sin and dragged it down into the gutters of vice. Two schools of thought emerged from this philosophy. One group became *ascetics;* those who, through harsh self-discipline and even self-mutilation, tried to curb the body's desires. Others became *hedonists.* They believed that, since only the soul would survive death, it didn't matter what was done through the body—so they gave the body every opportunity to quench its lustful thirsts. This hedonistic quest for pleasure gripped the sexually licentious city of Corinth and, unfortunately, also infected its Christian inhabitants.

1

## II. Liberty with My Body

When Paul taught on Christian liberty, the Corinthian believers mistook his instruction as an endorsement of their carnal lifestyle. They shouted "Amen" so loudly to the first part of this doctrine—in Christ we are free from serving the old master, the Law—that they drowned out the rest: in Christ we have been freed to serve a new master, God. They welcomed the idea that "all things are lawful for me" (1 Cor. 6:12), taking it for a banner to hang over their harmful justification of sexual immorality and other selfish desires (8:4–13, 10:23–33). What Paul said and what they heard were two different things. So he clears up the misunderstanding and poses two restrictions to keep Christian liberty within its proper bounds.

**A. Freedom within the limits of edification.** Paul sets the first boundary in 6:12a.

> All things are lawful for me, but not all things are profitable.[1]

Christians are indeed free from the Mosaic Law and its curse for disobedience (Gal. 3:10–14). But this liberty does not give us the right to do anything we please regardless of its effect on others. As Paul says,

> So then let us pursue the things which make for peace and the building up of one another. . . . Let each of us please his neighbor for his good, to his edification. For even Christ did not please Himself; but as it is written, "The reproaches of those who reproached Thee fell upon Me." (Rom. 14:19, 15:2–3)

**B. Freedom within the limits of self-control.** The Corinthians needed to learn that when they indulged their sinful desires, they were actually losing their freedom instead of enjoying it. Paul goes on to explain:

> All things are lawful for me, but I will not be mastered by anything. (1 Cor. 6:12b)

Paul wanted them to realize that when they didn't use their freedom to serve God, they unwittingly enslaved themselves to sin—they sold their freedom dirt cheap. So he encouraged them to refuse to be mastered by anything and to hang on to the precious freedom Christ had won for them.

---

### Whose Slave Are You?

The Corinthians were slaves of their own bodies, their own lusts.

---

1. *Profitable* comes from the word *sumpherō,* which literally means "to lift up together."

2

> Whose slave are you? Are you serving sex ... money ...
> ambition ... alcohol? Or, like Paul, are you a slave to God
> and righteousness (see Rom. 6:17–19)?
>
> Remember, whatever controls you, whatever drives you
> to keep living each day, masters you.
>
> It's not too late to change masters. The choice is en-
> tirely yours. What will it be? Whom will you serve?

## III. Purpose of My Body

Paul now subtly wedges into their hedonistic philosophy the truth of God's purpose for their bodies, sobering their playboy mentality.

**A. The Corinthian view.** The Corinthian Christians reasoned like this: when your body is hungry, feed it ... so, if your body has a sex drive, sate it! Notice how Paul breaks down their logic.

> Food is for the stomach, and the stomach is for food;
> but God will do away with both of them. (v. 13a)

Paul agrees that when they're hungry, they should eat. But he draws the line when they try to apply the same principle to the body and sexual fulfillment. The Corinthians didn't think it mattered how the body's sexual needs were gratified, since they thought that neither the body nor the sex drive would survive death—only the human soul would live on. But their conclusions didn't mesh with the Christian view.

**B. The Christian view.** Paul explains the right way to view the human body.

> Yet the body is not for immorality, but for the Lord;
> and the Lord is for the body. Now God has not only
> raised the Lord, but will also raise us up through His
> power. (vv. 13b–14)

Because our bodies will be resurrected, they should not be used for sexual immorality—whether premarital, extramarital, homosexual, bisexual, incestuous, or bestial. "The Lord is for the body"—He has purchased not only our souls but also our bodies from the slave market of sin (v. 20, 7:22–23; Titus 2:14; 1 Pet. 1:18–19). So we should serve God through our bodies, worshiping Him through obedience and abstaining from any form of sexual immorality.

## IV. Facts about My Body

In 1 Corinthians 6:15–20a, Paul continues to argue against the Corinthians' imbalanced views of the body and sex. He gives three facts about our bodies that further confirm their worth and our responsibility to use them for good.

**A. A physical extension of Christ.** With pungent sarcasm, Paul asks:

> Do you not know that your bodies are members of Christ? (v. 15a)

We are Jesus' representatives on earth. Like ambassadors in a foreign land who act as their nation's eyes, ears, hands, and mouth, we are Christ's ambassadors in this world, carrying out His interests in His name.

> **Ambassadors for Christ**
>
> God could have used mirrors to reflect His person... but He didn't. He could have sent angels to reveal His character... but He didn't. He gave that privilege to His children, to you and to me (see Eph. 6:19–20).
>
> What kind of ambassador are you? Have you learned the language of the lost—the syntax of their suffering, the nuances of their fears? And when you shake the hands of this world's citizens, do you reflect the warm, loving image of God Himself (compare John 13:34–35)?

**B. A moral illustration of the Lord's standards.** Paul explains in 1 Corinthians 6:15b–18 that we picture the Lord's holy standards in living color for all the world to see.

> Shall I then take away the members of Christ and make them members of a harlot? May it never be! Or do you not know that the one who joins himself to a harlot is one body with her? For He says, "The two will become one flesh."

When we have sexual relations outside of marriage, we form an immoral union that mars our holy alliance with God through Christ. But the Corinthians didn't believe this. They held that whatever was done by or through the body was not *immoral* but *amoral*—that is, morally irrelevant. Paul refutes their claim, saying, "the immoral man sins against his own body" (v. 18b). Sex outside of wedlock is wrong because it is a sin that abuses the body with pleasures that don't last and are ultimately vulgar sources of regret. So Paul commands us to "flee immorality" (v. 18a). We are not to be like Samson, who wasted himself in carnal relationships (Judg. 16), but like Joseph, who fled from the seduction of Potiphar's wife (Gen. 39).

> **Staying Pure**
>
> Purity starts in the mind. Solomon puts it this way, "For as [a man] thinks within himself, so he is" (Prov. 23:7a). In

Paul's first letter to the Thessalonians, he gives some advice for staying pure: "But examine everything carefully; hold fast to that which is good; abstain from every form of evil" (5:21–22).

Take a magnifying glass to your thought life. Are your thoughts making their home in the center of what is good, or are they camping dangerously close to borders that are improper, impure, or immoral? As Paul urges:

Finally, brethren, whatever is true, whatever is honorable, whatever is right, whatever is pure, whatever is lovely, whatever is of good repute, if there is any excellence and if anything worthy of praise, let your mind dwell on these things. (Phil. 4:8)

**C. A living temple of the Spirit.** Back in 1 Corinthians 6, Paul gives another reason for abstaining from sexual immorality.

Or do you not know that your body is a temple of the Holy Spirit who is in you, whom you have from God, and that you are not your own? (v. 19)

Just as the Lord manifested His presence in Solomon's majestic temple, setting it apart from all other buildings for special attention and use (2 Chron. 5:11–7:16), so the Spirit reveals His presence through us, ordaining and enabling us to bear His godly fruit in a wicked world (Gal. 5:16–24).

## V. Goal for My Body

Here's the bottom line of what Paul has been saying:

For you have been bought with a price: therefore glorify God in your body. (v. 20)

God let His Son die to redeem us from sin. One day, God will raise us from the dead, as He did with Christ Jesus, so we can reign with Him forever (vv. 2–3). In the meantime, the Lord expects us to live according to His standards. Why shouldn't He make this demand? He has bought us at the highest price, given us the noblest vocation, prepared for us the most glorious end. How can we do less than honor Him through obedience, especially through our bodies? Who are you serving with your body? If you belong to Christ, you should be serving Him. Are you? If not, flee the enslavement of immorality and run back to the liberating arms of Jesus. He alone is a worthy master, whose yoke is easy and whose load is light (Matt. 11:29–30). Come to Him if you're weary of the pain, heavy-laden with the guilt of immorality. He will give you rest (v. 28).

 *Living Insights*

In the first six chapters of 1 Corinthians, Paul rebukes the Corinthian church for their sinful condition. In chapter 7, he begins to answer a series of questions they had apparently asked in a previous letter. As we finish up chapter 6, let's look ahead and prepare ourselves for chapters 7–11, the ground we'll be covering in our study of *Practical Helps for a Hurting Church.*

• Read through 1 Corinthians 7–11. Find the questions that are asked in the text, and write them in the space provided. Don't worry about the answers at this point—we'll get to those in Study Two.

### 1 Corinthians 7–11

Verse: _____   Question: _____

_____

_____

Verse: _____   Question: _____

_____

_____

Verse: _____   Question: _____

_____

_____

Verse: _____   Question: _____

_____

_____

Verse: _____   Question: _____

_____

_____

Verse: _____   Question: _____

_____

_____

Verse: _____  Question: _____

_____

_____

Verse: _____  Question: _____

_____

_____

Verse: _____  Question: _____

_____

_____

Verse: _____  Question: _____

_____

_____

## 🦁 *Living Insights*

**Study Two** ▬▬▬▬▬▬▬▬▬▬▬▬▬▬▬▬▬▬▬▬

One of the best ways to motivate students is to arouse their curiosity. We hope the questions you found in Study One have made you wonder about their answers. Let's try to find some of them.

- Go back over your questions from the previous study. With your Bible open and ready for work, jot down the answers you find in each of these five chapters.

### 1 Corinthians 7–11

Verse: _____  Answer: _____

_____

_____

Verse: _____  Answer: _____

_____

_____

*Continued on next page*

7

Verse: _____    Answer: _____

_____

_____

Verse: _____    Answer: _____

_____

_____

Verse: _____    Answer: _____

_____

_____

Verse: _____    Answer: _____

_____

_____

Verse: _____    Answer: _____

_____

_____

Verse: _____    Answer: _____

_____

_____

Verse: _____    Answer: _____

_____

_____

Verse: _____    Answer: _____

_____

_____

# Single or Married—Which Is Better?

*1 Corinthians 7:1–7, 26, 35*

Winter 1984. Lake Placid, New York.

Whether you watched from the grandstands of the Olympic ice rink or the living room couch, most likely you were awed by the skaters' performances.

There were the Scott Hamiltons—the solo competitors, dynamos with uncanny strength and speed. Their aura of independence and determination was captivating. Inspirational. Their performances had a beauty all their own.

And there were the Tai Babilonias and Randy Gardners. Partners in the doubles competition glided across the ice, always aware of each other, supporting . . . dependent . . . every move contingent upon the move of the other. These duo performances graced the ice like no other. For they required the skill of skating in perfect sync with a partner.

How can you compare the two types of performances? Each had its own flare, its own purpose—and each drew a different audience.

As in the ice rink, in life there comes a time when we must choose to go solo or form a duo. Singleness or marriage. Which option is better for us? Which one will be more pleasing to the Judge?

Fortunately, we don't have to make this decision on our own. Paul coaches us, revealing God's guidelines on this important choice.

## I. Paul and Marriage: Some Introductory Questions

Before looking at what Paul says about marriage and the single life, we need to answer two questions that are commonly raised about him.

**A. Was Paul ever married?** Neither the New Testament nor extrabiblical literature answers this question conclusively. Scholars who think Paul was once married appeal to two strands of evidence.

1. **Jewish tradition.** In Paul's day marriage was expected among pious Jews when they reached the age of eighteen. "If a man did not marry and have children, he was to have 'slain his posterity,' 'to have lessened the image of God in the world.' "[1] Because Paul zealously upheld the orthodox

---

1. William Barclay, *The Letters to the Corinthians,* rev. ed., The Daily Study Bible Series (Philadelphia, Pa.: Westminster Press, 1975), p. 60.

traditions of his people (Acts 22:3, 26:5; Gal. 1:14), many believe he must have been married. Although strong, this argument does not prove that Paul had a wife. Jewish bachelors were present in the first century; for example, John the Baptist and Jesus. Perhaps Paul was also an exception to the norm. Also, if he had been married, why didn't he mention a wife when he counseled on marriage and family relationships?

2. **Membership in the Sanhedrin.** The second piece of evidence comes from his voting activity in the Sanhedrin.

> "And this is just what I did in Jerusalem; not only did I lock up many of the saints in prisons, having received authority from the chief priests, but also when they were being put to death I cast my vote against them." (Acts 26:10)

His power to vote shows that he was a member of this Jewish judicial body. And because members were required to be married and have children, Paul must have been a husband and a father.[2] However, the problem with this argument is that these rules weren't set until late in the first century or early in the second, many years after Paul's death.[3] While this fact doesn't demand that Paul was unmarried, it does show that, during his lifetime, his career didn't require marriage. So the jury is still out on the matter of Paul ever having a wife. But one thing is certain: by the time he penned 1 Corinthians, around A.D. 55, he was single (1 Cor. 7:7), and remained so until his death.

B. **Is Paul against marriage?** No way! In Ephesians 5:22–33, Paul compares marital love to the love Christ has for His Church; in 1 Timothy 4:1–3, Paul declares that the act of forbidding marriage will be a sign of end-times apostasy; and in 1 Corinthians 7:14, he even upholds the sanctity of mixed marriages— marriages between believers and unbelievers. Paul is definitely pro-marriage, but, as we'll see, he doesn't believe that marriage is for everyone.

## II. The Ideal Lifestyle

Paul opens 1 Corinthians 7 with the words "Now concerning the things about which you wrote." This phrase implies that the Corinthian believers had written to him about issues they were having

---

2. See *Letters to the Corinthians,* by Barclay, p. 61; and *Unger's Bible Dictionary,* 3d ed., by Merrill F. Unger (Chicago, Ill.: Moody Press, 1966), p. 838.

3. See *The Ministry and Message of Paul,* by Richard N. Longenecker (Grand Rapids, Mich.: Zondervan Publishing House, 1971), pp. 23–24.

problems with. Similar phrases throughout the rest of his letter show that this chapter on marriage and singleness marks the beginning of his direct replies to matters that greatly concerned the church at Corinth (see v. 25; 8:1; 12:1; 16:1, 12).

**A. The issue.** Paul responds to the Corinthians' first question, saying: "It is good[4] for a man not to touch a woman" (7:1b). Many have misinterpreted this statement, dubbing Paul a woman hater for two reasons. One camp takes this to mean that Paul feels marriage is either wrong or unprofitable; another, that he is encouraging sexual abstinence in marriage. The Corinthians represented both groups. In this letter Paul challenges the extremism in both views, but he never denies the value of the single life. In fact, he expresses his wish that all Christians were as he—unmarried.

> Yet I wish that all men were even as I myself am....
> But I say to the unmarried and to widows that it is
> good for them if they remain even as I. (vv. 7a, 8)

**B. The reasons.** One reason for staying single is given in verse 26.

> I think then that this is good in view of the present
> distress, that it is good for a man to remain as he is.

The "present distress" probably refers to the terrible persecutions Christians suffered at the hands of Roman officials.[5] Paul's advice is that in times of physical hardship, it's better to stay single and avoid the heartbreak of losing a loved one. Paul also says that singleness helps "secure undistracted devotion to the Lord" (v. 35b). Because singles do not have to work at meeting the desires and needs of a spouse, they can channel more of their energy into serving Christ. Their interests are not divided between God and mate; they can live for the Lord without having to synchronize their lives to their partners'.

## III. The Realistic Alternative

Although Paul prefers undistracted attention to the Lord over marriage, he realizes that many people need partners to go through life with. Not everyone is gifted to go it alone. Sexual immoralities lure many away from purity. So Paul tells them:

> But because of immoralities, let each man have his own
> wife, and let each woman have her own husband. (v. 2)

In this counsel Paul is not conveying a low opinion of marriage. It's important to remember that he's not writing a marriage manual, but answering questions in view of the Corinthians' tempting and tempestuous times. He's being realistic. As one commentary puts it:

---

4. *Good* means "morally excellent, wholesome." It conveys the image of that which is ideal.

5. See *Foxe's Book of Martyrs*, by John Foxe (Springdale, Pa.: Whitaker House, 1981), chap. 1.

In a society so full of temptations, he advises marriage, not as the lesser of two evils, but as a necessary safeguard against evil. So far from marriage being wrong, as some Corinthians were thinking, it was for very many people a duty.[6]

If you're single and find it difficult to control your sex drive, follow Paul's advice: seek out a partner, someone who will love you faithfully and fulfill your sexual desires within the bounds of marriage. Don't try to fulfill them while you're single. If you do, you will bring disharmony not only to your private life but also to your relationship with the Lord and fellow believers (see 1 Cor. 5:1–8, 6:15–19).

## IV. Sexual Fulfillment

Some of the Christians in Corinth didn't forbid marriage, but they did prohibit sexual intercourse between husband and wife. In response to this wrong thinking, Paul commands,

> Let the husband fulfill his duty to his wife, and likewise also the wife to her husband. (7:3)

The term translated *duty* means "debt." Jesus and Paul use this word in other contexts when referring to settling a bill with an individual or the government (Matt. 18:23–32, Rom. 13:7). Paul is saying that spouses are sexually indebted to each other and must regularly pay up. But what a wonderful bill to pay!

---

### The Beauty and Necessity of Sex

Throughout Scripture, the sexual relationship in marriage sparkles with pristine beauty (Prov. 5:15–19, Song of Solomon). As Mike Mason points out, this is for good reason:

> What can equal the surprise of finding out that the one thing above all others which mankind has been most enterprising and proficient in dragging through the dirt turns out in fact to be the most innocent thing in the world? Is there any other activity at all which an adult man and woman may engage in together (apart from worship) that is actually more childlike, more clean and pure, more natural and wholesome and unequivocally right than is the act of making love? For if worship is the deepest available form of communion with God (and especially that particular act of worship known as Communion), then surely sex is the deepest communion

---

6. Archibald Robertson and Alfred Plummer, *A Critical and Exegetical Commentary on the First Epistle of St Paul to the Corinthians,* 2d ed. (Edinburgh, Scotland: T. and T. Clark, n.d.), p. 133.

> that is possible between human beings, and as such
> is something absolutely essential (in more than a
> biological way) to our survival.[7]

Since sexual intimacy is so essential in marriage, couples need to ensure that their mates' physical needs are met. Remembering that their bodies belong to their mates will help (1 Cor. 7:4). Sexual gratification should not be withheld because of fatigue, apathy, boredom, resentment, or the like. Husband and wife have authority over each other's bodies. When one spouse needs or desires the deepest intimacies of love, the other spouse should delight in fulfilling that request. In verse 5, Paul gives only one exception to this rule; and, with it, he attaches three provisions. If these go unmet, sexual abstinence should not be practiced.

**A. Abstinence by mutual consent.** "Stop depriving one another, except by agreement for a time" (v. 5a). Husband and wife must agree, literally be "in symphony," that sexual relations should cease.

**B. Abstinence for an important reason.** ". . . That you may devote yourselves to prayer" (v. 5b). A couple should stop making love only when the reason is serious enough to drive them to their knees in prayer.

**C. Abstinence for a brief period.** "And come together again lest Satan tempt you because of your lack of self-control" (v. 5c). Stopping sexual activity is to be only temporary so that you won't be tempted to meet those physical needs outside the marriage relationship (see Prov. 5:15–19).

## V. Some Final Guidelines

Paul wraps up his counsel in verse 7:

> Yet I wish that all men were even as I myself am. However,
> each man has his own gift from God, one in this manner,
> and another in that.

Some of us are divinely equipped to remain single; others are suited for marriage. But how can we know if we are supposed to stay single or marry? The following biblical guidelines will help each of us come to an informed decision.

**A. It's better to remain single than . . .**

1. **To marry outside the Lord.** Choosing a non-Christian partner will always create relational problems far greater than those it solves.

---

7. Mike Mason, *The Mystery of Marriage: As Iron Sharpens Iron* (Portland, Oreg.: Multnomah Press, 1985), p. 121.

2. **To marry someone who will hinder our Christian growth.** Believers may marry other believers who will hamper their spiritual training. It's better for us to stay single than try to grow with partners who think they've learned all the spiritual skills they need.
3. **To marry for the wrong motive.** Marrying for money, power, prestige, fear of growing old alone, or simply because it's expected will inevitably lead to disaster. The only right reason to leave a single life is for love.
4. **To marry without being willing to give ourselves to another completely.** All of us are selfish to some degree. But if we are unwilling to sacrifice our own wants and needs for those of another every day for the rest of our lives, we shouldn't even entertain the idea of marriage.

**B. It's better to marry if . . .**
1. **Our lives would be more complete with a mate.** Unhappiness as a single may be a sign that God has not given us the gift of celibacy. Marriage will give us new motivation and joy.
2. **God leads us to someone we love and who loves us.** What greater proof do we need that we have found a life partner?
3. **We are confident that our relationship will illustrate Christ's love for His Church.** We do not really love enough to marry if our love is not sacrificial like Christ's. But if we are willing to give deeply of ourselves, we are ready to join lives with a partner.
4. **We are willing to spend the remainder of our days giving more than receiving.** Living successfully with a partner takes lots of time and practice ... practice ... practice! Like ice skaters who spend eight hours a day in the rink with their partners, falling and helping each other up and landing hard on the ice again, we've got to be willing to support our marriage partners (see Eccles. 4:9–10). Only if we are ready to consistently put out this kind of effort should we think seriously about marrying.

---
*An Absolute to Act On*

You may not yet know whether God has marriage in mind for you. Maybe that part of His will for you is still veiled ... maybe He's waiting for just the right time to show you.

---

> If you're in this position, just remember how much of God's will for your life you *are* sure about. And act on that. As Paul says:
>> For this is the will of God, your sanctification; that is, that you abstain from sexual immorality; that each of you know how to possess his own vessel in sanctification and honor. (1 Thess. 4:3–4)

 *Living Insights*

**Study One** ▬▬▬▬▬▬▬▬▬▬▬▬▬▬▬▬▬▬▬▬▬▬▬▬▬▬

Single or married—which is better? Has this lesson helped you answer that question? To round out our study, let's look at other Scriptures relevant to this topic.

- Let's compare the biblical accounts of a married couple and a single person. Read Genesis 2 and 3, and write down advantages and disadvantages to Adam and Eve's relationship. Then, for a slice of the single life, read Ruth 1 and 2, and jot down the advantages and disadvantages you find there.

| Single or Married—Which Is Better? | |
|---|---|
| Advantages | Disadvantages |
| Single | |
|  |  |

*Continued on next page*

| Advantages | Disadvantages |
|---|---|
| Married | |
| | |

# 🌼 Living Insights

**Study Two** ▬▬▬▬▬▬▬▬▬▬▬

Even though the struggles discussed in 1 Corinthians are more than nineteen hundred years old, many of them are still relevant today. The issue of singleness or marriage is one example. How does this relate to us in our day?

• In some instances it is better to marry, and in others, it is better to remain single. If you were in the position of providing counsel to a young person grappling with this issue, what advice would you give? Write out some of your thoughts in the space provided below.

**Single or Married?—My Counsel**

_____

_____

_____

_____

_____

_____

# God's Answer to the Unhappy Marriage

*1 Corinthians 7:8–16*

"To have and to hold from this day forward, for better, for worse, for richer, for poorer, in sickness, and in health, to love and to cherish, till death us do part."[1]

Are any words more tenderly holy than those of the marriage ceremony? And is there any union more deep and more joyous than that of a man and a woman becoming one flesh?

God designed marriage to be a delightfully intimate partnership (see Gen. 2:18, 24–25; Prov. 5:18–19), a union of warm innocence (see Heb. 13:4). He creates beauty in all things, and marriage is His masterpiece in the realm of relationships.

But just as the beauty of His holiness breathes things to life, so sin mars all with its cold death-touch. Like a butterfly's exuberant flight seared by a merciless sun—marriages are withered by sin...the one flesh is rent into two shredded and bleeding individuals.

Some mask the pain of their separateness by retaining the form of a marriage, living lives of "quiet desperation" as they plod through their days.

Others become angry, pounding out their differences through psychological or physical abuse. With howling hands they beat their spouses into submission; with brutal words they bludgeon them self-esteemless.

Separation offers escape—a respite from the hurt of a marriage gone bad. But a house divided cannot stand, and those who try to mend the broken pieces of their lives apart from each other seldom find the mutual solutions needed to reunite.

At the last, divorce hisses into the confusion; the serpent invades the Garden and drives relationships to dust.

These heartaches will not go away on their own. In 1 Corinthians 7:8–16, we'll see how God wants us to deal with these difficult situations.

## I. Answers for the Divorced and Widowed

The first situations addressed are those of the "unmarried" and "widows" (v. 8a). We know that widows are women who have lost

---

1. *Book of Common Prayer: Solemnization of Matrimony,* as quoted in *The Home Book of Quotations; Classical and Modern,* 10th ed., selected and arranged by Burton Stevenson (New York, N.Y.: Greenwich House, 1967), p. 1271.

17

their partners through death. But when Paul uses the word *un-married,* he is actually referring to those who have been divorced and are not yet remarried, rather than those who've always been single. Paul gives his attention to the needs of these vulnerable ones, seeking to show them their highest good through God's counsel.

**A. The ideal.** Singleness is the jewel in Paul's crown, as he says in verse 8:

> But I say to the unmarried and to widows that it is
> good for them if they remain even as I.

Paul would have the divorced and widowed remain single, not to inflict them with a life of loneliness, but to spare them the cares and worries involved in marriage. He'd like them to give their undivided attention to serving God (vv. 32–35).

**B. The concession.** Paul realized, however, that all divorced or widowed people do not have the gift of celibacy, not all are able to control their sexual passions. Of these Paul says, "Let them marry" (v. 9a).

**C. The reason.** Paul advises remarriage because "it is better to marry than to burn" with passion (v. 9b). Some people find it virtually impossible to subdue their sexual fires. So instead of being tormented or fulfilling their desires immorally, Paul tells them to remarry.

---

**Remarriage Reconsidered**

Along with Paul, Jesus allows remarriage in certain cases. Specifically, He permits remarriage for people who have divorced because their mates were unfaithful (Matt. 19:9).[2]

If you're a widowed or divorced Christian and contemplating remarriage, remember the boundaries set forth in Scripture. Follow the counsel Jesus and Paul give—and be sure to marry "only in the Lord" (1 Cor. 7:39b; see also 2 Cor. 6:14).

---

## II. Answers for the Married

In 1 Corinthians 7:10–16, Paul turns from the broken homes of the divorced and widowed to the fragile homes of the unhappily married.

**A. The ideal.** In verses 10–11, Paul states the Lord's ideal for the married:

---

2. The word Jesus uses to describe this immoral activity is *porneia,* which denotes not "a one-time-only experience" but "a sustained unwillingness to remain faithful ... an immoral *life style.*" From *Divorce,* by Charles R. Swindoll (Portland, Oreg.: Multnomah Press, 1981), p. 15.

> But to the married I give instructions, not I, but the
> Lord, that the wife should not leave her husband . . .
> and that the husband should not send his wife away.

Paul reaffirms what Jesus taught: Marriages are not seamed in heaven to be ripped out on earth. Mates are to cleave to each other, bond together, become one flesh—permanently. Christian couples should not give in to the destruction of divorce, but should do everything in their power to nurture and build their marriages.

**B. The concessions.** Unfortunately, this ideal cannot always be upheld in a sin-laden world. Paul doesn't hide from reality; instead, he gives us practical guidelines for handling painful situations God's way.

**1. Broken Christian marriages.** For Christians whose marital bonds have been severed by the sharp edge of selfishness, Paul gives these guidelines about remarriage:

> But if she does leave, let her remain unmarried,
> or else be reconciled to her husband. (v. 11a)

God wants the union of husbands and wives to endure; marriage is a sacred bond. If divorce occurs, they should either stay single or start fresh with each other—not with anyone else. But Christians may marry people other than their former partners when their divorce was caused by sexual immorality (Matt. 19:9). Even when this exception applies, though, believers are free to remarry only other believers (see 1 Cor. 7:39b, 2 Cor. 6:14).

**2. Continuing mixed marriages.** What about marriages in which only one mate is a believer? Should these unions continue, or should spiritual incompatibility allow them an end? Jesus never addressed this issue while on earth; however, Paul provides us with spiritually sound advice based on his God-given authority.

> But to the rest I say, not the Lord,[3] that if any
> brother has a wife who is an unbeliever, and she
> consents to live with him, let him not send her
> away. And a woman who has an unbelieving hus-
> band, and he consents to live with her, let her
> not send her husband away. (vv. 12–13)

**3. Spiritually mixed marriages that fail.** The last situation Paul deals with concerns marriages in which the non-Christian

---

3. Paul's phrase "I say, not the Lord" doesn't mean that he was giving his own opinion on the issue. Rather, it means that his convictions weren't based on any former direct command from the Lord.

spouse leaves—literally "separates from" or "divorces"—the Christian mate. As Paul says:

> Yet if the unbelieving one leaves, let him leave;
> the brother or the sister is not under bondage
> in such cases, but God has called us to peace.
> (v. 15)

The saved partner hasn't prompted or encouraged the split; the lost mate just wants out. Paul's advice is "let him leave"—don't fight it, just let go. The Christian is the victim of a willful desertion and is "not under bondage in such cases." In other words, the child of God is no longer enslaved to that relationship, but becomes the "unmarried" person spoken of in verse 8. For our heavenly Father finds great delight in giving us peace, not misery, and if unmarried Christians find happiness in remarrying, they're free—*only in the Lord* (vv. 9, 39)!

**C. The reasons.** Why should Christians strive to keep their marriages to unbelievers intact? Paul gives three reasons.

1. **Sanctification of the unsaved spouse.** Just as Laban's household was blessed because of Jacob (Gen. 30:27) and Potiphar's because of Joseph (39:5), so non-Christian mates are blessed because of their Christian spouses. Also, a believer is Christ's representative in the home, exposing the unbeliever to the very person of the Lord Jesus Christ. The lost mate is sanctified—set apart—because of God's presence in the life of the believing partner (1 Cor. 7:14a).

2. **Spiritual cleansing of the children.** Christian parents who bring up their children according to God's standards will have a spiritual impact on their lives. Their children will learn how to discern right from wrong and will take with them a knowledge of God's grace (v. 14b).

3. **Salvation of the unbelieving mate.** The fact that one partner in a marriage is saved indicates that God is at work in that marriage. By remaining committed to that union and to godliness, Christian mates can greatly influence their unbelieving partners to turn their lives over to Christ (v. 16; compare 1 Pet. 3:1–2).

---

### Some Marital Counsel

Although Scripture allows for divorce under certain circumstances, it never encourages it. Divorce, the defeat of love, should only be pursued when all other approaches have led to dead ends.

---

Are you contemplating divorce as the way out of your marital problems? If so, ponder these words from Mike Mason before making a final decision:

> Couples who begin to feel themselves "out of love" need to return to doing the sort of things they did together when they *were* in love.... Originally we did these things only with the help of God's gift of ... natural attraction.... But God is not interested, ultimately, in natural attraction. He wants us to come to know the supernatural attraction of His Own sort of love. So later in life, we may be called upon to repeat ... our original acts of love ... but this time without much help from the emotions.... We may be called upon to act all alone, out of pure faith and trust, perhaps without even the perceived help of our partner. For it is often God's way that what He Himself has taught us to do in the light, we must repeat on our own in the darkness.[4]

## III. Dealing with the Divorced

Before we move on, we need to spot-check our attitude toward the divorced. Too often, we treat these hurting brothers and sisters as if they had committed the unpardonable sin. We cut them off from the ministries and social circles they once enjoyed. We leave them to grieve their losses and piece together their lives ... alone. And when we find ourselves in their company, we frequently look for the nearest exit. Remember, divorce is forgivable, and, as Christians, we are to be a forgiving people—people who console and reconcile, not condemn and chastise. Divorced Christians need our love, our embraces, our encouragement, our time. Let's not forsake them. Let's accept them with open, forgiving arms ... as Christ does us.

*Continued on next page*

4. Mike Mason, *The Mystery of Marriage: As Iron Sharpens Iron* (Portland, Oreg.: Multnomah Press, 1985), pp. 95–96.

 *Living Insights*

Unhappy marriages. What should be done about them? The only sure counsel comes from Scripture. The Bible gives us at least five crucial passages on marriage, separation, divorce, and remarriage. Let's dig into them so we can better understand God's mind on these issues.

- Does the Bible allow for divorce? If so, under what circumstances? What about remarriage? What does God's Word say about issues like these? Use the space provided to record the principles of marriage, separation, divorce, and remarriage found in the passages listed.

### Marriage, Separation, Divorce, and Remarriage

Genesis 2:18–25 _____

_____

_____

_____

_____

Deuteronomy 24:1–4 _____

_____

_____

_____

_____

Matthew 19:3–12 _____

_____

_____

_____

_____

Ephesians 5:22–33 _____

_____

_____

_____

_____

1 Peter 3:1–7 _____

_____

_____

_____

_____

 *Living Insights*

Do you know of some marriages that are in trouble? Unfortunately, most of us can compose quite a list. Have you given any thought recently to what *you* could do to help? Remember, you can always pray.

• Devote this Living Insights time to showing your concern for the troubled marriages you are aware of. If you know how you can help, start helping. If not, spend this time in prayer for these people. Never underestimate the power of prayer. Many times it is the only way to discover God's answer to an unhappy marriage.

# Biblical Advice on Staying Single

*1 Corinthians 7:25–35*

Somehow, the grass always seems greener on the other side of the fence. Like fielded cows, we poke our heads past our barbwire boundaries to graze in another's pasture—where the grass seems to taste so much better than ours. But if we were to stop . . . and listen, we'd hear others' chomps as they grazed on our grass, leaving *their* green fields for still other dissatisfied souls.

You've heard them. Husbands and wives up to their elbows in garage grease, dirty dishes, and Tinkertoys, saying, "If only I had more time to myself. Then I could accomplish some of my goals . . . then I'd feel worthwhile."

And just down the street, single people, settled into the careers of their dreams, home at 5:30 every day to Lean Cuisine and the news—wishing they had someone to eat dinner with and someone else's voice besides Dan Rather's to listen to.

Too many look at their lives and see only the weeds. But in 1 Corinthians 7:25–35, Paul encourages us to look at the green grass instead. He advises those on both sides of the fence, but especially singles, to stay where they are and graze—contentedly.

## I. Some Advantages of Singleness

Paul's advice to singles can be nutshelled in these words: *Staying unmarried is desirable, but it isn't demanded.* He backs up this point with four advantages singles have that married people don't. Although Paul's thoughts are not drawn from Jesus' teaching, they have been revealed to Paul by the Holy Spirit and are just as authoritative as Christ's words (v. 25; compare v. 40; 2 Pet. 1:21, 3:15b–16).

### A. Singles will encounter less distress from a hostile world. 
Paul writes, "I think then that this is good in view of the present distress, that it is good for a man to remain as he is" (1 Cor. 7:26). Even though persecution was sporadic and localized in Paul's day, he believed it was only a matter of time before Christians throughout the Roman Empire would suffer for their faith. And he was right. About ten years after he wrote 1 Corinthians, the Roman emperor, Nero, falsely blamed Christians for setting the imperial capital ablaze. He slaughtered believers of all ages; one rampage followed another, spilling over Rome's city limits into the rest of the empire. The persecution of Christians was horrible. They were punished with

> stripes and scourgings, drawings, tearings, stonings,
> plates of iron laid unto them burning hot, deep

dungeons, racks, strangling in prisons, the teeth of
wild beasts, gridirons, gibbets and gallows, tossing
upon the horns of bulls. Moreover, when they were
thus killed, their bodies were laid in heaps, and dogs
there left to keep them, that no man might come to
bury them.[1]

It's probably difficult for most of us to relate to stonings and
scourgings, dungeons and racks. But what about twentieth-
century hardships—the loss of a job, a reputation, a mate, a
child? It is because believers still face the brunt of the world's
hostility toward Christ that Paul's advice to stay single applies
to us today. Suffering alone is difficult enough, but watching a
mate or a child suffer with you can be unbearable. Paul's advice
is to stay on your side of the fence: if you are already married,
stay married. But if you're single, the threat of persecution and
hardship should discourage you from seeking a husband or wife
(v. 27).

**B. Singles will experience fewer difficulties on a per-
sonal level.** Because Paul was emphasizing so strongly the
value of staying single, the Corinthians might have begun to
think that marriage was sinful. So he tells them:

But if you should marry, you have not sinned; and if
a virgin should marry, she has not sinned. Yet such
will have trouble in this life, and I am trying to spare
you. (v. 28)

Many unmarried people look at singleness and see only the
weeds. But the large number of divorces today is a telltale sign
that marriage provides anything but an idyllic pasture of green
grass. Certainly, marriage yields many rewards, but the process
is costly. It increases our responsibilities; it calls for readjust-
ments to our finances, leisure time, and personal goals. But
more than anything else, it grates against our selfishness. As
Mike Mason explains:

Marriage comes with a built-in abhorrence of self-
centeredness. In the dream world of mankind's com-
placent separateness, amidst all our pleasant little
fantasies of omnipotence and blamelessness and self-
sufficiency, marriage explodes like a bomb. It runs
an aggravating interference pattern, an unrelenting
guerrilla warfare against selfishness. It attacks
people's vanity and lonely pride in a way that few
other things can, tirelessly exposing the necessity of
giving and sharing, the absurdity of blame. Angering,

---

1. John Foxe, *Foxe's Book of Martyrs* (Springdale, Pa.: Whitaker House, 1981), p. 18.

humiliating, melting, chastening, purifying, it touches us where we hurt most, in the place of our loveless- ness. Dragging us into lifelong encounters which at times may be full of boredom, tension, unpleasant- ness or grief, marriage challenges us to abandon everything for the sake of love.[2]

The single life also confronts our egos, but without the struggles a mate adds to it.

C. **Singles can expect fewer distractions from time spent on spiritual matters.** Paul says that "the time has been shortened" (v. 29a), probably referring to the amount of time left before the Rapture. He also writes, "the form of this world is passing away" (v. 31b)—this earth is deteriorating while it awaits its destruction and re-creation by God (Rom. 8:19–22, 2 Pet. 3:10–13, Rev. 21:1). Understood together, these two verses urge Christians to invest their time in eternal matters, for time is brief and the world corrupt. And those with time wrapped up in family, pleasures, and possessions are distracted from spiri- tual priorities (1 Cor. 7:29b–31a).

---

### A Note of Clarification

Again, Paul isn't saying that the concerns which accom- pany marriage are sinful. He's just exposing some of mar- riage's weeds. Let's face it. Single people have more time for activities like evangelism, discipleship, and prayer.

If you're single, is there a missionary endeavor, an internship, a church involvement you can do that you couldn't if you were married? If so, take advantage of the time God's given you to serve Him undividedly.

---

D. **Singles can enjoy greater concentration in their rela- tionship with God.** Married couples are rightly concerned about cultivating their marriages and satisfying their spouses' needs and desires. The unmarried, on the other hand, are able to give their undivided attention to the Lord. As Paul says:

> But I want you to be free from concern. One who is unmarried is concerned about the things of the Lord, how he may please the Lord. . . . And the woman who is unmarried, and the virgin, is concerned about the things of the Lord, that she may be holy both in body and spirit; but one who is married is concerned about

---

2. Mike Mason, *The Mystery of Marriage: As Iron Sharpens Iron* (Portland, Oreg.: Multnomah Press, 1985), p. 45.

the things of the world, how she may please her
husband. (vv. 32, 34b)

And to clear up any possible misunderstanding, Paul explains
his ultimate goal for them one more time.

And this I say for your own benefit; not to put a restraint upon you, but to promote what is seemly, and
to secure undistracted devotion to the Lord. (v. 35)

---

### *"Undistracted Devotion"*

To put it bluntly, many singles aren't interested in being
completely devoted to the Lord.

They may be so afraid that if they give up pursuing a
mate, they'll never get married; so they just keep living by
their own desires and drives.

Or they may be afraid that if they get too close to Him,
He'll alter their life's goals, send them to Africa as mission-
aries—that somehow He'll make them accept their singleness and muffle their cry for a mate.

What we all need to remember is that He wants complete devotion—He wants us to love Him with all our
hearts ... all our souls ... all our minds ... and all our
strength (Mark 12:30).

---

## II. Some Commands for Singles

If you're single, Paul's words are addressed to you. As we worked
our way through them, maybe you realized that you have not spent
your time as you should. Maybe you began to see that the attention
you've given to your career or finding a mate has been misdirected.
If your response to singleness has been unbiblical, you can turn it
around and make it count for Christ by following three one-word
commands.

**A. Rejoice!** Thank God for your singleness, and enjoy it as His
best for you at this time in your life. He is in control of your
circumstances. If and when He wants them to change, He will
bring it about.

**B. Reverse!** Rechannel your energies. Instead of using them to
look for a marriage partner or advance your career, use them
to give yourself totally to God, fulfilling His desires as if He were
your earthly beloved.

**C. Relax!** Quit hungering for the grass on the other side of the
fence. Stay in your pasture—yes, even though you're alone—
and feed on the many benefits God has for you there. The pasture of singleness can be a pasture of contentment if you'll
rejoice, reverse, and relax.

 *Living Insights*

First Corinthians 7:25–35 is rich in practical helps. It's the kind of chapter that needs to be studied carefully so we don't miss important information. Let's use the method of paraphrasing and spend some extra time in this passage.

● Are you familiar with this method? It allows you to get acquainted with the verses and gives you a chance to read between the lines. While putting Paul's words into your own, you'll discover some feelings you never felt before.

**1 Corinthians 7:25–35**

_____

_____

_____

_____

_____

_____

_____

_____

_____

_____

_____

_____

_____

_____

_____

_____

_____

_____

_____

_____

_____

_____

_____

 *Living Insights*

**Study Two** ━━━━━━━━━━━━━━━━━━━━━━━━

Being single today brings with it a whole set of benefits and complications. Get together with a group of friends and discuss issues facing singles, using the following questions as a guide. Encourage openness and try to get everyone involved.

- What pressures are experienced by singles? Does our culture make it harder or easier? Why?

- How can the single life be positive?

- Where does God's will fit into all of this?

# Love, Liberty, and the Meat Problem
*1 Corinthians 8*

One of the most penetrating statements that ever fell from Jesus' lips was this:

> "Love one another, even as I have loved you.... By this all men will know that you are My disciples, if you have love for one another." (John 13:34b–35)

Notice what He didn't say and the words sink in even deeper.

He didn't say that all men will know we are His disciples if we become serious students of the Word ... or if we fast once a week ... or attend every conference and seminar held in our city ... or even if we give our time, talent, and money to God's work.

All of these things are valuable, commendable parts of every growing Christian's experience, but not one of them is the magnet that draws people to a knowledge of God. Only when the world sees the love in the family of God will they be drawn into the Father's arms.

True love—*agapē* love—was sorely lacking in the Corinthian church, and this was affecting their attitudes toward all kinds of issues. The issue Paul addresses in 1 Corinthians 8, Christian liberty in relation to meat sacrificed to idols, serves as an anvil upon which he hammers out his instruction.

## I. The Cultural Problem
The hot issues in the Corinthian church weren't whether or not to go to the movies, play cards, or drink wine with dinner. Instead, they worried about the correctness of eating meat that had been sacrificed to idols. Remember, Corinth was a center for idol worship. As a part of this worship, an animal was brought before a priest to be sacrificed. Only parts of the animal were burned; the leftovers were either divided among the priests and city officials or sold in public marketplaces. This was a problem for believers, because when they bought meat, chances were good that some of it came from a false god's barbecue. Add to this the public banquets following the sacrifices and the private dinner parties featuring idol-meat casserole, and the Corinthian Christians were in a sticky situation![1] Some

---

1. One commentator explains this knotty dilemma: "The believers of Corinth and the other Greek cities found themselves in a difficult position in regard to the heathen society around them. On the one hand, they could not absolutely give up their family and friendly relations;

*Footnote continued on next page*

argued that eating the meat sacrificed to idols wasn't wrong; others, that it was as bad as idol worship itself. Undecided, they brought the issue to Paul and plopped in his lap the burden of resolving it.

---

**— Paul's Challenge ——————————————**

Frederic Godet, in his commentary on 1 Corinthians, explains the challenge Paul faced this way:

The solution of these questions bristled with difficulties. The one party held strongly to their liberty, the other not less seriously to their scruples. The apostle must avoid favouring either superstition in the latter or libertinism in the former. He needed all his practical wisdom and all his love to trace a line of conduct on this subject which would be clear and fitted to unite hearts, instead of dividing them.[2]

---

## II. The Biblical Solution

Because this issue of eating meat sacrificed to idols is so complicated, Paul spends chapters 8, 9, and 10 addressing it. This lesson will cover only chapter 8, where Paul attempts to nail down the ideal of a genuine love that is willing to restrict its liberty.

**A. The principle of liberty.** The Corinthians knew they were free in Christ. But many of them took this to an extreme, thinking that Christian liberty was their ticket to sin (compare 1 Cor. 6:12, 10:23). Paul is quick to straighten out their twisted thinking, reminding them of two guidelines they already knew.

**1. They knew they had knowledge.** Paul begins chapter 8 by setting up a contrast between knowledge and love.

Now concerning things sacrificed to idols, we know that we all have knowledge. Knowledge makes arrogant, but love edifies.[3] (v. 1)

---

the interests of the gospel did not allow them to do so. On the other hand, these relations were full of temptations and might easily draw them into unfaithfulnesses, which would make them the scandal of the Church and the derision of the heathen." From *Commentary on First Corinthians*, by Frederic Louis Godet (1889; reprint, Grand Rapids, Mich.: Kregel Publications, 1977), p. 401.

2. Godet, *Commentary on First Corinthians*, p. 403.

3. The Greek word for *edifies* "is *oikodomeō*, which literally means 'build a house,' and so more generally 'build.' One could translate the last part of this verse: 'Knowledge blows up, but love builds up.' The first verb is *physioō*, which comes from *physa*, 'bellows.' So it means 'blow up' or 'inflate.' " Ralph Earle, *Word Meanings in the New Testament* (Grand Rapids, Mich.: Baker Book House, 1986), p. 230.

Paul states that every believer has knowledge, a God-given window of reality through which to view life. He's not knocking that. He is, however, warning against having a knowledge untempered by love. This kind of knowledge inflates our egos, making it impossible for us to build up others.

---

**A Note on Edification**

Knowledge blows up, but love builds up. As Ralph Earle explains, the picture in verse 1

> is a striking contrast. Intellectualism often inflates a person with pride. We can blow up a balloon in a minute or two, and collapse it in a second with a pin prick. So it is with self-important intellectuals. They can be deflated with a single remark.
>
> But building up with love is something else. Just as one has to lay stone on stone or brick on brick in order to construct a solid building, so we must lay one loving deed on another if we would build a solid life that will last.[4]

What about you? Is your church, your school, your home a knowledge factory—cranking out facts, facts, facts that rarely impact your life? Remember, knowledge without love only tears down (see 1 Cor. 13:2b), and we are in the building-up business.

---

2. **They knew about idols.** Paul brings them back to the issue of eating meat, reminding them of another important aspect of their knowledge.

> Therefore concerning the eating of things sacrificed to idols, we know that there is no such thing as an idol in the world, and that there is no God but one. For even if there are so-called gods whether in heaven or on earth, as indeed there are many gods and many lords, yet for us there is but one God, the Father, from whom are all things, and we exist for Him; and one Lord, Jesus Christ, by whom are all things, and we exist through Him. (8:4–6)

Paul's logic is clear. Since idols are merely man's creation . . . since there is really only one true God (v. 6), eating meat

4. Earle, *Word Meanings in the New Testament,* p. 230.

that has been sacrificed to idols is in itself inconsequential. After all, how can meat be made evil by gods that don't exist?

**B. The principle of love.** Paul appeals not only to the Corinthians' knowledge and logic but also to their responsibility to love weaker believers—those who are saved but untaught, ignorant of their liberty, easily offended, and preoccupied with appearances.

> However not all men have this knowledge; but some, being accustomed to the idol until now, eat food as if it were sacrificed to an idol; and their conscience being weak is defiled. (v. 7)

Some believers didn't understand that the meat issue wasn't immoral but amoral—morally neutral—and that eating the meat would not affect their relationship to Christ (v. 8). So Paul tells the Corinthians to put a lid on their liberty around these people.

> But take care lest this liberty of yours somehow become a stumbling block to the weak. For if someone sees you, who have knowledge, dining in an idol's temple, will not his conscience, if he is weak, be strengthened to eat things sacrificed to idols? For through your knowledge he who is weak is ruined, the brother for whose sake Christ died. (vv. 9–11)

Again, Paul emphasizes that knowledge can tear down, ruin, stumble the unstable off their feet (v. 11). But when tempered by love, it can edify (v. 1).

## III. Our Response

So what is to be our loving response? Paul's answer is firm:

> Therefore, if food causes my brother to stumble, I will never eat meat again, that I might not cause my brother to stumble. (v. 13)

Paul isn't talking about tiptoeing around the legalistic scruples of sanctimonious believers, those who have made Christianity a meticulous system of law. He's talking about protecting the tender conscience of a weak believer. In a nutshell he's telling us that *the extent of our love is determined by the attitude with which we restrain our liberty.*

---

**Liberty or Love?**

Even though we don't have to battle the issue of eating meat sacrificed to idols, our culture is sprayed with gray areas that threaten to taint the black-and-white.

---

When you face issues like dancing, drinking, watching movies, which is your priority: exercising your Christian liberty, or practicing Jesus' love? Do you view weaker believers as nuisances, in the way of your liberty's independent exercise? Or do you see them as an opportunity to show an interdependent love—one that encourages, accepts, and respects others?

Regardless of our differing stances on the gray issues of life, we have all been called to obey one command that stands crisp and clear in black and white: "Love one another" (John 13:34b).

##  Living Insights

**Study One** ▬▬▬▬▬▬▬▬▬▬▬▬▬▬▬▬▬▬▬▬▬

Liberty. We all want it, but getting it in this imperfect world can be a difficult quest. In New Testament times the big taboo was eating meat offered to idols. Few of us struggle with that issue today. But there are plenty of other issues roadblocking our path toward liberty.

- Do you understand 1 Corinthians 8? Take a few minutes to reread the thirteen verses. Then read them in another version. This should help you glean insights that you never noticed before.

##  Living Insights

**Study Two** ▬▬▬▬▬▬▬▬▬▬▬▬▬▬▬▬▬▬▬▬▬

OK, so you don't struggle over meat sacrificed to idols. But before you pat yourself on the back, is there another area of life and liberty that causes you discomfort? What is your twentieth-century taboo? And how are you dealing with it? Use the space provided to record your answers to these questions.

- What specific areas of liberty do I struggle with?

_____

_____

_____

_____

_____

_____

- How have I dealt with these areas in the past?

  _____

  _____

  _____

  _____

  _____

  _____

- Based on this study, what are some effective ways of dealing with these issues?

  _____

  _____

  _____

  _____

  _____

  _____

# Bottom of the Ninth, Score's Tied, You're Up

*1 Corinthians 9:1–23*

Picture it. You're a member of a baseball team playing its most important game of the season. It's the bottom of the ninth. The score is tied, the bases are loaded, and you're up to bat. Taking a few practice swings on your way to the batter's box, you look down at the third-base coach for the signal. Expecting a "swing away" sign, you begin to churn inside when he dips his hat, licks his thumb . . . when he begins to give the "sacrifice" signal. What? Fly out on purpose so our team can score? What about my .350 batting average?

And so, you're faced with a choice. Will you sacrifice, or risk losing the game to go for a grand slam? Will you play for your own glory, or for the glory of the team?

As we've already seen, the Corinthian team suffered from individualism. They viewed themselves as distinct, isolated players and gave little thought to how their actions would affect the rest of the team. In 1 Corinthians 9:1–23, Paul shows us the individualistic attitudes they practiced, and then, in a dugout talk, he exhorts them to be team players for the Lord.

## I. Paul's Position

The Corinthians had been liberated by Christ to live in freedom (compare Gal. 5:1), and they were intent on exercising their new-found rights. This sounds healthy, as if they were living the promised abundant life and discovering the fullness of God's grace. However, if there was a backward way to do something, the Corinthians found it. They had taken their freedom and fed their egos with it—they spent their liberty on self. Rather than bolstering their team members, they fought for their own rights. Paul challenges this individualistic attitude by highlighting his own position as an apostle. After all, if every Christian has rights, then certainly apostles have more because of their status in the Church. Paul asks:

> Am I not free? Am I not an apostle? Have I not seen Jesus our Lord? (v. 1a)

After listing his unique credentials, he continues:

> Are you not my work in the Lord? If to others I am not an apostle, at least I am to you; for you are the seal of my apostleship in the Lord. (vv. 1b–2)

Not one of the Corinthian believers could argue with that. If it hadn't been for Paul's ministry in their city, they would still be lost. If anyone had the right to do as he pleased when up to bat, it was Paul.

36

## II. Paul's Rights

Just in case someone might doubt his privileges as an apostle, he lists several of them.

> Do we not have a right to eat and drink? Do we not have a right to take along a believing wife, ... or do only Barnabas and I not have a right to refrain from working? (vv. 4–6)

This last right—full financial support from local churches—is the focus of the rest of Paul's appeal. He defends this claim, asking three rhetorical questions.

> Who at any time serves as a soldier at his own expense? Who plants a vineyard, and does not eat the fruit of it? Or who tends a flock and does not use the milk of the flock? (v. 7)

Paul sharpens his point with Scripture, finding support from another man of God, Moses:

> For it is written in the Law of Moses, "You shall not muzzle the ox while he is threshing." God is not concerned about oxen, is He? Or is He speaking altogether for our sake? Yes, for our sake it was written, because the plowman ought to plow in hope, and the thresher to thresh in hope of sharing the crops. If we sowed spiritual things in you, is it too much if we should reap material things from you? (vv. 9–11)

Paul is like the Old Testament priest, commissioned by God to practice and proclaim His Word. Just as priests were to be supported for their ministry, so the Lord directed Paul to "get [his] living from the gospel" ministry (vv. 13–14).

## III. Paul's Sacrifice

Although Paul was fully entitled to exercise his rights, he chose to sacrifice them for the team's sake. He opted to "endure all things" so that he would not cause any "hindrance[1] to the gospel of Christ" (v. 12b). Paul's sacrifice is admirable, but we might ask why he refused to accept even the bare necessities of life from the churches he served. William Barclay provides a possible answer:

> While the ordinary Jewish family ate meat at the most once a week the priests suffered from an occupational disease consequent on eating too much meat. Their privileges, the luxury of their lives, their rapacity were notorious; Paul knew all about this. He knew how they used religion as a means to grow fat; and he was determined that he would go to the other extreme and take nothing. . . .

---

1. In Greek, *hindrance* is a surgical term for making an incision. In using this word, Paul expresses that he didn't want his financial needs to cut into the body of Christ.

In the last analysis one thing dominated his conduct. He would do nothing that would bring discredit on the gospel or hinder it. Men judge a message by the life and character of the man who brings it; and Paul was determined that his hands would be clean. He would allow nothing in his life to contradict the message of his lips. Someone once said to a preacher, "I cannot hear what you say for listening to what you are." No one could ever say that to Paul.[2]

Even though he had the right to grab some glory for himself, Paul always surrendered his gratification for the good of Christ's team. Did Paul benefit from doing this? Absolutely!

What then is my reward? That, when I preach the gospel, I may offer the gospel without charge, so as not to make full use of my right in the gospel. (v. 18)

For Paul, this was reward enough.

---

### Star or Team Player?

If you're a Christian, you have the right to use your liberty and position in Christ to enjoy all God has for you. But you also have the responsibility and privilege of building up other Christians in the faith. That takes teamwork, which calls for personal sacrifice (compare Eph. 4:1–16). Are you willing to forfeit your rights, to give up the chance of being a star, so you can help your fellow believers grow as a team?

If so, watch out! Your decision will not be an easy one to carry out. Many people, even fellow teammates, have imbibed the world's approach to life. If you wish to become rich, they will urge you to hoard your money. But God will encourage you to give it away, making you more wealthy than you ever imagined. The world will try to exploit your desire to become a leader, advising you to take charge and rule with an iron fist. But the Lord would have you lead by serving, to win others through humility and gentleness. Because it's in this way that you will one day rule the world with Christ.

Each day you will have to choose how you'll play the game of life—the Christian life. Will you play as a star or a team player? The decision is a tough one, but it's one that must be made—every time you're up to bat.

---

2. William Barclay, *The Letters to the Corinthians,* rev. ed., The Daily Study Bible Series (Philadelphia, Pa.: Westminster Press, 1975), p. 81.

## IV. Paul's Goal

Paul is concerned about the team's goal—winning souls for Christ as well as strengthening fellow team members. He makes this clear in verse 19:

> For though I am free from all men, I have made myself a slave to all, that I might win the more.

Paul develops this thought further in verses 20–22. Even though he has both Christians and non-Christians in mind, we'll apply this to Christians only. This will help us understand our teammates more clearly and enable us to do what it takes to hit them in to home plate.

**A. To win Christian legalists.** On first base are those believers who live under a rigid system of dos and don'ts. They haven't yet grasped their liberty in Christ. To free them, we first may have to submit to their moral standard. As Paul explains:

> And to the Jews I became as a Jew, that I might win Jews; to those who are under the Law, as under the Law, though not being myself under the Law, that I might win those who are under the Law. (v. 20)

Because of Paul's restraint, many under the Law were brought above it to enjoy the full knowledge of Christ.

**B. To win Christian libertines.** The freedom abusers stand on second. They use their Christian liberty in ways that dishonor God and hurt their teammates. To correct them, Paul encourages mobility in method, but not in morals. He urges us to associate with these believers—not compromising our standards but winning them over with love (v. 21).

**C. To win Christian babes.** Those waiting on third base are the spiritually immature. They are easily offended, and their tendency to slip back into sin runs high. More than anything else, they need mature believers to teach them Christianity's essentials and help them apply those truths to life. To begin this training process, we may have to restrain our liberty, at least while we're with them. As Paul explains:

> To the weak I became weak, that I might win the weak; I have become all things to all men, that I may by all means save some. And I do all things for the sake of the gospel, that I may become a fellow partaker of it. (vv. 22–23)

---

### Strike Out or Sacrifice?

A hush falls over the dugout. All eyes are on you. Your teammates wonder if Paul's talk has convinced you to sacrifice. The umpire breaks the silence: "Play ball!" You're up. What will you do? Will you yield your rights to bring

---

as many runners home as you can? Or will you ignore Christ's call to sacrifice and risk losing the game for the sake of your ego? We, your teammates, need your help to win. Won't you give it—for the team?

 *Living Insights*

**Study One**

Throughout 1 Corinthians, Paul has a lot to say about love, liberty, and unity. And he continues these thoughts as he develops the ninth chapter. His comments on these subjects, however, are not limited to 1 Corinthians—this theme appears in some of his other letters as well.

● Let's glean some principles on love, liberty, and unity from two of Paul's other epistles. Study Romans 12 and Ephesians 4:1–16. Then in the chart below, list the principles you discover.

| Love, Liberty, and Unity | |
|---|---|
| Passages | Principles |
| | |
| | |
| | |
| | |
| | |
| | |
| | |
| | |

*Living Insights*

As was so clearly stated in this study, a spirit of independence or individualism can severely weaken a team. The team that usually comes out on top is the one whose members are unselfish, united in purpose, willing to sacrifice their rights so that the ultimate goal of winning can be achieved.

● Are you committed to unity? How do you demonstrate it in your life? How can you improve in this area? Write down the answers to these questions in the space provided.

**My Commitment to Unity**

_____

_____

_____

_____

_____

_____

_____

_____

_____

_____

_____

_____

_____

_____

# In the Arena
*1 Corinthians 9:24–27*

Every four years, millions of lives revolve around the event that cele-brates the height of athletic achievement: the Olympics. Spectators capsize their routines so they can watch their favorite athletes compete. And the athletes make their final preparations, polishing their routines and running through their strategies for the millionth time; the sweat-and-tears award dangling like a carrot before their minds' eye.

The smell of victory is in the air. And the image in everyone's mind is a three-tiered stand, with the winner exalted on the highest tier, proudly wearing the gold medal.

In contrast to all the hoopla surrounding the Olympics, little attention is paid to the years of rigorous training that produce a winner. Champions aren't born, they're made. And the tools that forge them are discipline, motivation, and realistic goals.

What's true for athletes in the Olympic Games is true for Christians in the arena of life. Without the right training, desire, and objective, victory will always be out of reach. So what is the formula for becoming a winner? The Lord tells us through the words of Paul. Let's listen closely to our trainer. If we follow His advice, one day we'll stand as victors before His throne.

## I. The Scene
The core of our training manual is 1 Corinthians 9:24–27. These verses drip with the sweat of athletes. You can almost hear their grunts and groans as you read this text. But you'll never fully under-stand these verses until you grasp their key term and cultural back-ground.

**A. The key word.** The crucial term in this passage is *self-control* (v. 25). It means "strength within," carrying the idea of mastering oneself instead of giving in to impulse or overindulgence. In this context, it gives the key to victory in the Christian life: discipline.

**B. The central event.** Paul is speaking from the grandstands of the Isthmian games—his equivalent of our Olympics. Held every two years ten miles outside Corinth, these games brought people from every part of the Mediterranean to compete or just to watch. It was the sporting event of the year, drawing the empire's finest talent. Athletes would compete in foot races, broad jump-ing, discus throwing, wrestling, boxing, gymnastics, and eques-trian contests. The athletes competed fiercely, each one striving for the coveted Isthmian crown—a wreath of wild celery. Win-ners also received lifetime exemptions from paying taxes and serving in the military, tuition-free educations, and statues of themselves erected along the roadway that led to the site of the games. But the real prize was the celery wreath, awarded to each winner at the end of the games.

## II. The Scripture

While reflecting on the Christian life, Paul draws from his memories of the games to teach us how to become spiritual victors.

**A. A question and a command.** Paul opens with a rhetorical question that sends his speech off and running.

> Do you not know that those who run in a race all run, but only one receives the prize? (v. 24a)

Paul isn't talking about salvation, but rewards. Not all Christians will be rewarded for the way they lived their lives. Some will appear before Christ's judgment seat expecting a pat on the back for a job well done. But when their works are tested with fire, they will all be burned to ashes. These believers will never receive crowns from the Lord for faithful service. Other Christians, however, those who faithfully obey His Word, will be rewarded for the spiritual good they accomplished on earth (3:13–15, 2 Cor. 5:9–10). So Paul encourages us, saying, "Run in such a way that you may win" (1 Cor. 9:24b). Paul wants us to realize that running just to finish the race will never bring a reward . . . it takes keeping the goal in mind—and going all out—to get it.

---

*Remember the Prize!*

You might be wondering who would run a race with anything in mind *but* winning . . . who would train all that time expecting to lose, content to go home empty-handed. *We* would, spiritually speaking. And we do it all the time.

We forget our purpose—winning the race for the sake of Christ's glory—and we just run. Unprepared, fatigued, muscles taut, wearing our hiking boots, still we run, as if we've forgotten about the prize.

> We go and take our place in the course as though the prize could be won without any running at all, or as if there were no prize worth running for. We dream and loiter and fold our arms; we turn aside to look at every object of passing interest; or if we did begin with some vigour, all the zest and warmth of the struggle grows feebler and fainter when it ought to become more animated, and . . . we care little

---

what hindrances occur to stop our course, and
to risk a dishonourable fall.[1]

Runners for Jesus, remember the goal! Remember the
prize! As the writer of Hebrews says, "Lay aside every
encumbrance, and the sin which so easily entangles us,
and let us run with endurance the race that is set before
us" (Heb. 12:1).

**B. The preparation and the prize.** To give it our best, we must
be properly trained. This involves "self-control in all things"
(1 Cor. 9:25a). The Isthmian athletes submitted themselves to a
grueling training program that called for long hours, a strict
diet, abstinence from alcohol, and almost masochistic exercise
sessions. They endured all this with one goal in mind: winning
a wreath . . . one that would last only a brief time. Paul shows
us that, unlike the ancient athletes, we run for eternal gold.

They then do it to receive a perishable wreath, but
we an imperishable. (v. 25b)

Since those athletes disciplined themselves so strenuously for
a wilting wreath, how much more should we train to win an
indestructible reward?

---

### Settling for the Perishable

C. S. Lewis gives his thoughts on our easy-chair attitude
toward God's rewards:

If we consider the unblushing promises of reward and the staggering nature of the rewards
promised in the Gospels, it would seem that
Our Lord finds our desires, not too strong, but
too weak. We are half-hearted creatures, fooling
about with drink and sex and ambition when
infinite joy is offered us, like an ignorant child
who wants to go on making mud pies in a slum
because he cannot imagine what is meant by
the offer of a holiday at the sea. We are far too
easily pleased.[2]

How about you? Are you too easily pleased with the
temporal, investing your training time in winning withering

---

1. John S. Howson, *The Metaphors of St Paul,* 2d ed. (London, England: Strahan and Co., 1869), p. 153.

2. C. S. Lewis, *The Weight of Glory and Other Addresses* (Grand Rapids, Mich.: William B. Eerdmans Publishing Co., 1949), pp. 1–2.

> celery-wreath awards? Or are you training hard for the day
> when Jesus will hang the precious gold around your neck?

**C. The method and the motivation.** In verses 26–27, Paul
stops using the plural term "we" and, using himself as a model,
starts talking "I":

> Therefore I run in such a way, as not without aim; I
> box in such a way, as not beating the air. (v. 26)

When Paul ran the spiritual race, he didn't stop to pick the
daisies—he always kept the goal in mind, always kept his eyes
glued to the tape. And when he was in the ring with sin, he
rarely threw a wild punch. When he cocked back his fist and
swung, he landed squarely on target. Sin is relentlessly decep-
tive, constantly working to catch us off guard to knock us to the
canvas. The only way we can win is to dodge its swings and
plant our punches firmly on target, like Paul. And that takes
discipline—the kind of self-control that beats us black-and-blue,
if it has to, so we can leave the ring on our feet. Paul states it
this way:

> I beat my body and make it my slave so that after I
> have preached to others, I myself will not be disquali-
> fied for the prize. (v. 27)[3]

We dare not let down our guard against sin. We must have a
strategy to defeat it in our lives, objectives we can achieve in
God's power that will weaken our opponent and eventually send
it reeling.

## III. The Significance

Paul has given us a great deal to think about, but let's not leave it
in the realm of the mental. Let's examine our lives to see how we're
holding up against three brutal boxers that bludgeon us in the ring.
Our goal is to discover where we lack self-restraint so we can become more effective fighters for the Lord. All three problem areas
are discussed in 1 John 2:16.

**A. "The lust of the flesh."** This opponent is the craving for
sensuality. In the Old Testament, sensuality was represented by
the idol Ashtoreth. Her followers worshiped her through every
form of sexual perversity imaginable. Although today we don't
have any temples in her honor, she is alive and well in our
sex-obsessed culture. Has she delivered an uppercut to your
life? Has she dizzied you with pornography, premarital sex,

---

3. *The NIV Study Bible* (Grand Rapids, Mich.: Zondervan Bible Publishers, 1985). For a detailed
study of eternal rewards, read *Grace in Eclipse,* by Jane C. Hodges (Dallas, Tex.: Redencion
Viva, 1985).

adultery, or homosexuality? Don't let down your guard! She only wants to flatten you. See her as the empty idol she really is. Turn back to God, and let Him take control of your sexual passions.

**B. "The lust of the eyes."** This opponent is the equivalent of the ancient idol Baal—the god of materialism. He promised wealth and success to anyone who revered him. Has he caught you off guard? Have you taken your eyes off Christ and placed them on things? Is possessing more important to you than giving? If so, realize that you have become an idolater. You cannot serve the true God and a false god at the same time. Step back and regain your balance. Don't allow Baal to steal your eternal crown.

**C. "The boastful pride of life."** The Old Testament god that symbolized this sin was Molech, the god of influence. Many people thought he would give them power if they fed his ego with the lives of their children. How important is your pride? Are you willing to sacrifice the good of others, even of your family and friends, to gain self-recognition and influence? If so, Molech has landed a destructive blow to your life. You can stop him from doing any further damage if you'll sacrifice your ego to the Lord and let Him build you up in the image of Christ (see Eph. 4:15–16, Rom. 8:29).

---

### Winning the Fight in the Arena of Your Heart

If God were to open the door to the private arena of your heart, would He find an Ashtoreth, a Baal, a Molech winning the match? If so, ask Him to give you the self-control to knock them out of your life. He *will* give it (see Mark 11:24). He longs for you to be a winner so you can honestly echo Paul's words: "I have fought the good fight, I have finished the course, I have kept the faith" (2 Tim. 4:7).

---

 *Living Insights*

**Study One** ▬▬▬▬▬▬▬▬▬▬▬▬▬▬▬▬▬▬▬▬▬▬

The passage we are studying is brief—only four verses—but it's action-packed! When looking at the parts of speech that give a text its power, pay attention to the verbs. Let's take a closer look at these action words.

- Reread 1 Corinthians 9:24–27. In the space provided, write down all the verbs that are in the passage. Then go back over the text and find a definition of the verb. Finally, jot down the significance of the term—why it's important to the passage.

## 1 Corinthians 9:24–27

Verb: _____

Definition: _____

Significance: _____

_____

Verb: _____

Definition: _____

Significance: _____

_____

Verb: _____

Definition: _____

Significance: _____

_____

Verb: _____

Definition: _____

Significance: _____

_____

Verb: _____

Definition: _____

Significance: _____

_____

Verb: _____

Definition: _____

Significance: _____

_____

*Continued on next page*

Verb: _____

Definition: _____

Significance: _____

_____

Verb: _____

Definition: _____

Significance: _____

_____

Verb: _____

Definition: _____

Significance: _____

_____

Verb: _____

Definition: _____

Significance: _____

_____

Verb: _____

Definition: _____

Significance: _____

_____

Verb: _____

Definition: _____

Significance: _____

_____

## 🐎 *Living Insights*

*An idol . . . anything that takes the place of God in your life.* Though most of us don't think of ourselves as idolaters, when it's defined this way, more of us qualify than would like to admit. What is your idol?

• This lesson ended with three areas of struggle. Rather than answering yes or no to these idols, use the following scale to rate the degree of struggle you face.

---

Are you preoccupied by lust, yearning to fulfill the sensual drives within?

    Hardly at all    Somewhat    More than average    Greatly

Reason for your rating:

---

Are you overly attracted to or absorbed by things?

    Hardly at all    Somewhat    More than average    Greatly

Reason for your rating:

---

Are you lost in your drive for power, influence, or prestige?

    Hardly at all    Somewhat    More than average    Greatly

Reason for your rating:

---

If you didn't score too well in one of these areas, take a little time right now to develop a plan of action that will put God back on the top of your heart's altar.

# Please Follow the
# Instructions . . . or Else!
*1 Corinthians 10:1–11*

Eleven o'clock Christmas Eve. The children are all tucked in bed, at least pretending to be asleep, and you're faced with the task of assembling the electric train you hope will steam "Merry Christmas" around the tree in the morning.

You drag the box out from under the bed and read the bold black writing on its side: INSTRUCTIONS INCLUDED. Anxious to see what you're in for, you open the box. To you, the parts seem simple enough, the assembly process logical enough—so you toss the instruction booklet aside, roll up your sleeves, and go for it on your own.

Two hours later, just out of curiosity, you reach for the instruction booklet and are horrified to find that the diagrams look nothing like the mess you have in front of you. So, realizing that your sanity is far more valuable than your pride, you take the whole thing apart and start from scratch—this time with the instructions.

When it comes to assembling an electric train, this independent, I'll-do-it-my-way attitude is relatively harmless; you can always tear the thing apart and start over. But when it comes to real issues instead of playthings, the consequences can be irrevocable.

As we've seen, the Corinthian believers were assembling their lives without following God's instructions and were ending up with a hideous mess. So, using the example of the Hebrews in the wilderness, Paul urges them to stick to the guidelines God had given them to live by.

## I. Privileges Experienced by the Hebrews
In 1 Corinthians 10:1–11, Paul spins the wheel of time backward to a spoke of the past—to the day of the Hebrews' wilderness wanderings. He saw that this spoke in the cycle of history had wheeled around to touch the earth the Corinthians walked on,[1] for the believers at Corinth needed to learn much the same lesson as the children of Israel. Neither of them could blame their failure to follow God's guidelines on receiving unclear instructions; both were wealthy with privileges that encouraged them to live godly lives. In verses 1–4, Paul concentrates on five of the Hebrews' great privileges.

**A. Supernatural guidance.** Although they might have felt as if they were wandering aimlessly, the Hebrews were not without a guide. As Paul says:

1. See Ecclesiastes 1:3–11 for a biblical reference to the cycles of time.

50

> For I do not want you to be unaware, brethren, that
> our fathers were all under the cloud. (v. 1a)

The cloud he's referring to is the "pillar of cloud by day" and the "pillar of fire by night" that led them in their journey to the Promised Land (see Exod. 13:21). Twenty-four hours a day they could look up and see either the cloud or the fire and know whether God wanted them to move to the right or to the left, stop and pitch their tents or pull up the stakes and go. For them it was no guessing game—following His guidance was as simple as opening their eyes.

**B. Supernatural deliverance.** Paul also says that the Hebrews "passed through the sea" (1 Cor. 10:1b). Exodus 14:21–22 gives us the historical account.

> Then Moses stretched out his hand over the sea; and
> the Lord swept the sea back by a strong east wind
> all night, and turned the sea into dry land, so the
> waters were divided. And the sons of Israel went
> through the midst of the sea on the dry land, and the
> waters were like a wall to them on their right hand
> and on their left.

Every physical law says they all should have drowned. Yet, because of God's intervention, not even their feet got wet.

**C. Supernatural leadership.** Another of the Hebrews' privileges was the godly leadership they enjoyed under Moses.

> And all were baptized into Moses in the cloud and in
> the sea. (1 Cor. 10:2)

This doesn't mean that Moses held a baptismal service. *Baptize* comes from the Greek word *baptizō,* which carries the idea of identifying with something else.[2] In Paul's day if you wanted to have a garment dyed a different color, you would take it to a merchant who would "baptize" it—dip it to change its identity. The Israelites had been spiritually dipped into a union with God, Moses, and Moses' leadership. Notice how they responded to his godly guidance:

> And when Israel saw the great power which the Lord
> had used against the Egyptians, the people feared
> the Lord, and they believed in the Lord and in His
> servant Moses. (Exod. 14:31)

---

2. As one commentator explains: " 'They were all baptized into Moses in the cloud and in the sea' simply means they were initiated and inaugurated under God into union with him and also with Moses and his leadership. Compare the expression 'baptized into Christ' (Rom. 6:3,4; cf. Gal. 3:27; and see Heb. 3:1–6)." From *The Expositor's Bible Commentary,* 12 vols., ed. Frank E. Gaebelein (Grand Rapids, Mich.: Zondervan Publishing House, 1976), vol. 10, p. 249.

**D. Supernatural food.** In 1 Corinthians 10:3, we read that they "all ate the same spiritual food." Paul is referring to the manna that God supplied for the Hebrews for forty years, six days a week, so that they never went hungry (Exod. 16:4–36; Ps. 78:24–25, 29). Terming the food "spiritual," Paul implies that it was to be a means of grace to God's people. This food was not only physically nourishing to the Hebrews but also a symbol of the body of Christ, which would be broken for them to restore their souls (see Luke 22:19, Isa. 53:5).

**E. Supernatural drink.** With the food came the privilege of God-sent water.

> And all drank the same spiritual drink, for they were
> drinking from a spiritual rock which followed them;
> and the rock was Christ. (1 Cor. 10:4)

Here's a perfect illustration of the preincarnate presence of the Lord Jesus. Even before He took on human flesh, He had His hand in the affairs of His people—in this case, providing them with all the water they needed (see Exod. 17:1–7).

---

*A Thought to Consider*

The cloud ... deliverance from the sea ... leadership ... food ... drink. Every one of these privileges was much more than the provision of a physical need. Every one of them was an act of grace.

In our lives, too, there is no gift, no blessing, no privilege we enjoy that meets *only* a surface need. With each kindness He shows us—even in tiny acts of provision—He brushes us with a touch of His salvation. If you'll just sit still and wait, you'll feel them ... subtle stirrings of His grace all around you.

---

## II. Lessons for the Corinthians

You'd think that a people as blessed as the Hebrews would have responded to God with thankfulness and obedience. But that wasn't the way it went in the wilderness. After listing their many blessings, Paul explains:

> Nevertheless, with most of them God was not well-pleased;
> for they were laid low in the wilderness. (1 Cor. 10:5)

Out of the hundreds of thousands of Israelites in that first generation, only Joshua and Caleb pleased God. The rest of their bodies were strewn across the wilderness floor. As Frederic Godet states: "What a spectacle is that which is called up by the apostle before the eyes of the self-satisfied Corinthians: all those bodies, sated with miraculous food and drink, strewing the soil of the desert!"[3] Why does Paul mention this? He tells us himself:

> Now these things happened to them as an example,[4] and they were written for our instruction,[5] upon whom the ends of the ages have come. (v. 11)

He wanted to show us through the Hebrews' example that having privileges doesn't guarantee successful living; you need to open God's instruction booklet to correctly assemble a godly life. Paul gives five directions.

**A.  Do not crave evil things.** The first step to God's instructions is found in verse 6:

> Now these things happened as examples for us, that we should not crave evil things, as they also craved.

Paul starts off small—with an attitude, a craving for evil. The Israelites had been overexposed to supernatural benefits, yet they lacked the proper response. Dissatisfied and ungrateful in the face of vast blessings, they kept longing to go back to Egypt (see Num. 11:4–6).

**B.  Do not be idolatrous.** His second instruction is "do not be idolaters, as some of them were" (1 Cor. 10:7a). An idol is anything that seizes the adoration that belongs to God. It can be a parent, a child, a spouse, a friend, a reputation, a goal . . . *anything* that takes God's seat on the throne of our hearts.

**C.  Do not become immoral.** "Nor let us act immorally, as some of them did," Paul says (v. 8a). The idea here is to not *become* immoral, suggesting a process. It begins with an evil attitude, continues with a substitution of other things in God's place, and results in immorality—anything in our lives that's inconsistent with purity.

**D.  Do not try the Lord.** Questioning God's faithfulness in providing for them, the Hebrews asked: " 'Why have you brought us up out of Egypt to die in the wilderness?' " (Num. 21:5a). And God's response was not a warm one (see v. 6). So Paul warns us:

> Nor let us try the Lord, as some of them did, and were destroyed by the serpents. (1 Cor 10:9; see also Ps. 78:40–41)

3. Frederic Louis Godet, *Commentary on First Corinthians* (1889; reprint, Grand Rapids, Mich.: Kregel Publications, 1977), pp. 487–88.

4. *Example* comes from the Greek word *tupos*, which means "to strike with a blow for the purpose of leaving an impression." It's the same word used in John 20:20, 25, and 27 for the nail prints in Jesus' hands. It was also used in biblical days for stamping the imprint of the emperor on coins. Therefore, Paul is saying that the wilderness incidents should make a strong, permanent impression on us.

5. *Nouthesia,* Greek for *instruction,* means "to put or set into the thinking to change one's behavior."

Daring God to come through on His promises shows a lack of faith and, from the looks of what happened to the Hebrews, is a serious thing in God's eyes.

**E. Do not grumble.** Finally, there was a brash, caustic reaction that poured from the Hebrews' hearts. When they didn't get what they wanted, they complained—bitterly and relentlessly (see Num. 16:41; 17:5, 10). The last instruction Paul gives is not to "grumble, as some of them did" (1 Cor. 10:10a). For their thankless grumbling, God judged the Hebrews harshly (v. 10b).

---

*A Quick Trek through the Wilderness of Your Heart*

In that dry, desolate desert of your heart, is a piece of your character lying parched in a pit? A prickly attitude sprouting the spines of sin? A patch blooming with idolatry, immorality, or mistrust? A gritty, grumbling spirit that rubs God wrong?

Just remember God's responses to the Hebrews' wilderness sins—they were severe and unalterable. But don't let this keep your heart wandering fearfully. Let it drive you to Jesus, the oasis, where you can find the water of forgiveness and rest (see John 4:14, Matt. 11:28).

---

## III. Lessons We Can Apply

Even in the presence of great privileges and blessings, the Hebrews refused to follow God's instructions. Why? Because the supernatural had become ordinary; they took God's presence for granted. And like a supersaturated sponge that never gets squeezed, they spoiled. We struggle with the same problem of overexposure to the things of the Lord. Especially if we live in a Christian home, attend Christian schools, and are involved in Christian activities. It's easy for the doldrums to set in . . . the boring, grinding, day in, day out of the Christian life.

**A. Signs of spiritual saturation.** It's not difficult to spot believers who are spiritually calloused. Among other things, they have an overriding spirit of negativism, a preoccupation with petty irritations, a lack of vision, a prideful attitude, and an inappropriate sense of humor—especially concerning spiritual things.

**B. Curing spiritual saturation.** If your spiritual sponge can't hold another drop of God's truth, here are some instructions to help make you right with Him. First, recognize, confess, and forsake whatever is keeping you from God. Second, deal severely with your inner attitudes. Go beneath the mask; tear off your

Sunday face. Look at yourself on Thursday afternoon. Third, listen to what you're saying. Pay attention to your choice of words. Are they cutting, cynical, bitter, coarse (see Luke 6:45)? And fourth, discover and cultivate every possible way to keep your life fresh and vital.

> **A Final Thought**
>
> Jesus summarizes the whole point of this lesson in Luke 12:48b:
>
>> And from everyone who has been given much shall much be required; and to whom they entrusted much, of him they will ask all the more.
>
> The Hebrews . . . the Corinthians . . . us. We all are prime examples of people God has seen fit to privilege. And all He asks in return is a gracious spirit and an obedient heart.

 *Living Insights*

**Study One** ▬▬▬▬▬▬▬▬▬▬▬▬▬▬▬▬▬▬▬▬▬▬▬▬▬▬▬▬▬▬▬▬

One of the most exciting aspects of personal Bible study is to see Scripture overlap. This text in 1 Corinthians is a great example. There Paul constantly refers to the Old Testament, specifically the story of Moses and the children of Israel.

- Using the chart that follows, examine closely the Old Testament passages mentioned in our study. As you dig into them further, write down what you find in these cross-referenced texts.

| Cross-referencing 1 Corinthians 10 ||
|---|---|
| Exodus 14:21–22 | 1 Corinthians 10:1b |
| | |

*Continued on next page*

| Exodus 14:31 | 1 Corinthians 10:2 |
|---|---|
| | |

| Exodus 16:4–36 | 1 Corinthians 10:3 |
|---|---|
| | |

| Exodus 17:1–7 | 1 Corinthians 10:4 |
|---|---|
| | |

| Numbers 21:5–6 | 1 Corinthians 10:9 |
|---|---|
| | |

| Numbers 16:41 | 1 Corinthians 10:10 |
|---|---|
| | |

## Living Insights

Attitude . . . idolatry . . . immorality . . . distrust . . . causticity.  These were the five stages the Hebrews experienced in their rebellion against God. And they're the same ones we find ourselves in today.

• Do you have a person you're accountable to? If so, take this opportunity to share these stages of rebellion with them. Ask them to honestly evaluate where *you* are in this struggle. Be prepared to hear some hard stuff. Hopefully, this will be a memorable time of sharing because of the solutions you'll find.

# Idol Altars and Demon Activity Today

*1 Corinthians 10:12–22*

C. S. Lewis explains the shocking similarity between sins of action and sins of thought:

> [Christian writers] seem to be so very strict at one moment and so very free and easy at another. They talk about mere sins of thought as if they were immensely important: and then they talk about the most frightful murders and treacheries as if you had only got to repent and all would be forgiven. But I have come to see that they are right. What they are always thinking of is the mark which the action leaves on that tiny central self which no one sees in this life but which each of us will have to endure— or—enjoy—forever. One man may be so placed that his anger sheds the blood of thousands, and another so placed that however angry he gets he will only be laughed at. But the little mark on the soul may be much the same in both. Each has done something to himself which, unless he repents, will make it harder for him to keep out of the rage next time he is tempted, and will make the rage worse when he does fall into it. Each of them, if he seriously turns to God, can have that twist in the central man straightened out again: each is, in the long run, doomed if he will not. The bigness or smallness of the thing, seen from the outside, is not what really matters.[1]

Why can a tiny sin of thought that seems so harmless be just as dangerous as a blatantly malicious one? Because there is a progression in sin. If unerased, the "little mark on the soul" left by a sin of the mind will smear— until one's character is permanently stained (see James 1:15).

Sometimes it's best to stay away from something for the simple fact that being associated with it could lead you into trouble. As a "harmless" thought can lead to a heinous sin, so a "harmless" association can lead to spiritual disaster.

## I. Words for a Few

The Corinthians were headed for just such a disaster. In the name of celebrating their liberty, they participated in idolatry, which, as Paul explains, is just one curve on the downward spiral into the pit of demonism.

---

1. C. S. Lewis, *The Joyful Christian* (New York, N.Y.: Macmillan Publishing Co., 1977), p. 163.

**A. The self-confident.** Paul first warns the proud Corinthians who, with pompously upturned noses, felt they could never fall through the manhole into the sewer of sin.

> Therefore let him who thinks he stands take heed lest he fall. (1 Cor. 10:12)

The word *heed* means "to look at something." Paul is saying, "If you're so sure you'll stay standing, take a closer look . . . realize that you—yes, even you—might be headed for a fall" (compare Prov. 16:18). So Paul warns them to guard against this haughty spirit by seeing themselves realistically—vulnerable, dependent on God, able to fall.

**B. The discouraged.** Not all the believers at Corinth were self-righteous. Some felt overwhelmed and overcome by temptation. To them Paul brings a word not of caution but of comfort.

> No temptation[2] has overtaken you but such as is common to man; and God is faithful, who will not allow you to be tempted beyond what you are able, but with the temptation will provide the way of escape also, that you may be able to endure it. (1 Cor. 10:13)[3]

---

### Comfort for Us

Do you ever feel completely alone in the temptations you wrestle with? Ever think that if faced with them just one more time, you'll crash and burn? During those times, remember Paul's soothing words—words that will help cool the heat of any temptation, if you'll let them.

Remember, *no* temptation is uncommon; we're all in the same fire. And *He is faithful* to provide the way of escape and give strength to endure the searing licks of temptation's white-hot flame (see 1:9, 2 Pet. 2:9).

---

2. To clarify a point of possible misunderstanding, the kind of tempting talked about in 1 Corinthians 10:13 is very different from the tempting spoken of in James 1:13–14. In James, the temptation is a solicitation to evil. God has no part in this. But in 1 Corinthians, the testing is to prove our strength, to make us grow—it's something definitely designed by God.

3. Many commentators interpret this verse differently, feeling that it is directed to the whole body of Corinthian believers and is to be taken not so much as a word of encouragement but as an emphatic reaffirmation of the need for vigilance. They would give it this meaning: " 'Take so much the more heed as you are not yet out of danger. Up till now you have not been very greatly tempted . . . but how will it be if there should come on you stronger temptations than the former? God no doubt will still protect you, but on condition that you watch.' " From *Commentary on First Corinthians,* by Frederic Louis Godet (1889; reprint, Grand Rapids, Mich.: Kregel Publications, 1977), p. 497.

## II. Warning for All

The Corinthians desperately needed this encouragement, for they had chosen to live on the unraveling fringe of the Christian experience. Living dangerously close to the pagan world, they surrounded themselves with all its temptations. So Paul puts up a stop sign; because if they kept going in the same direction, what had begun as a celebration of liberty would have ended as a lamentation of bondage to sin.

**A. The command.** So far, Paul has just been warming up. But from here on out, almost without a transition, his admonitions are unswerving and direct.

> Therefore, my beloved, flee from idolatry. (1 Cor. 10:14)

An idol is anything that constantly pulls your heart from the Lord, that constantly wants to be enthroned in His place (see Rom. 1:21–23, Isa. 44:9–20).

---

**Something to Think About**

Idols.

Israel made hers out of gold, wood, and stone.

What about you? Have you made yours out of the flesh of another person . . . the paper of money . . . the warm, woolly security blanket of a happy home?

These things may not be evil in and of themselves—in fact, they may be very good things—yet when exalted, they become idolatrous.

---

**B. The reasons.** Paul felt strongly about this issue because he understood its implications. He knew that the Corinthians' association with idolatry would lead to grieving God's heart and destroying their fellowship with Him. To support his command, he tells them why it's so important to flee idolatry.

  1. **Association with idolatry leads to participation in idolatry.** Through two examples—the Lord's Table and the nation of Israel—Paul shows us how this first step toward spiritual disaster happens.

     > Is not the cup of blessing which we bless a sharing in the blood of Christ? Is not the bread which we break a sharing in the body of Christ? Since there is one bread, we who are many are one body; for we all partake of the one bread. Look at the nation Israel; are not those who eat the sacrifices sharers in the altar? (1 Cor. 10:16–18)

     Notice that the idea of *sharing* comes up in this passage three times. Paul's point is that by associating ourselves with the body and blood of Christ when we take communion, we become participators with Him—we enjoy His fellowship and a union with other believers. Also, the Israelites were able to participate with God in fellowship and worship through their sacrifices (see Deut. 12:18). It was Jesus, the unseen reason behind the Lord's Supper, and Jehovah, the unseen reason behind the sacrifices of Israel, who made these things meaningful. And as Paul's logic implies, it is Satan, the unseen force behind idolatry, who makes it so destructive.

2. **Participation in idolatry leads to involvement with the devil.** Taking them back to the issue he discussed in chapter 8, Paul clarifies his warning:

> What do I mean then? That a thing sacrificed to idols is anything, or that an idol is anything? No, but I say that the things which the Gentiles sacrifice, they sacrifice to demons, and not to God; and I do not want you to become sharers in demons. (1 Cor. 10:19–20)

There is nothing wrong with the stone or wood of an idolatrous altar, or even the meat offered to idols. But what *is* dangerous is the force of darkness, the demonic world, that hides behind the visible stuff of idols.[4] When you get too deeply entrenched in a certain sin, an idol is created. And once an idol is carved, Satan has gained a foothold in your life and can begin his takeover.

3. **Involvement with the things of the devil leads to spiritual disaster.** The kernel of the problem is that you can't be involved with Satan and the Lord at the same time. Like oil and water, the two just don't mix.

> You cannot drink the cup of the Lord and the cup of demons; you cannot partake of the table of the Lord and the table of demons. (v. 21)

God won't tolerate split loyalties. He wouldn't in Israel's day (see vv. 5–10, Deut. 32:21–25, Ps. 78:54–64), and He won't in ours.

---

4. "It is a great mistake to imagine that back of their idolatry and their idol sacrifices there is nothing but an empty vacuity. True enough, ... the gods of the idols have no existence whatever. ... But something does exist, something that is far more terrible than these pseudo-gods, namely an entire kingdom of darkness which is hostile to God, a host of demons ... who are ruled by the greatest of their number, namely Satan." From *The Interpretation of St. Paul's First and Second Epistle to the Corinthians,* by R. C. H. Lenski (Columbus, Ohio: Wartburg Press, 1946), p. 415.

## III. Some Warnings for Us

Satan is alive and well—brilliantly scheming to attack you[5] (see 2 Cor. 2:11, 1 Pet. 5:8). Just as the forces of heaven are active, so are the forces of hell. And there is nothing that would stop the devil, short of your denial of the faith. Every association with wrong, every "little mark" on your soul, Satan will highlight again and again until your testimony for Jesus is completely stained. That's his delight.

**A. Satan's goal.** Satan delights in Christians who love to live on the No Trespassing borders of carnality—those who value their liberty above their loyalty to Christ. In camping so near to enemy territory, they make themselves highly vulnerable to his attacks.

**B. Satan's attacks.** God has made us with minds, emotions, and wills. And Satan attacks us in each of these areas. He entices our intellects with false religions, parapsychology, palmistry, and ESP—every kind of unbiblical philosophy. He also ravishes our emotions with a lust for the sexually perverse—pornography, homosexuality, masochism, and bestiality. And he overthrows our wills, inciting us to rebel against authority.

---

### *"Greater Is He . . ."*

When talking about the relentless attacks of Satan, we easily get a victim complex about ourselves . . . easily forget all about our responsibility over our own minds, hearts, and wills. Just remember, *we choose* to live either righteous or carnal lives. But we're certainly not abandoned, left to grope our way on our own. It is through the power of Jesus that we are able to renounce our sins—our alliances with Satan—and be restored to fellowship with God.

What sins have given Satan a foothold in your life? What idols are crowding out the Lord on the throne of your heart? If God is speaking to you today, go ahead . . . make things right with Him. Renounce those sins. And He will give you the strength to overcome. For "greater is He who is in you than he who is in the world" (1 John 4:4b).

---

5. If you would like to be better equipped in the battle against Satan, the following sources will be helpful: *I Believe in Satan's Downfall,* by Michael Green (Grand Rapids, Mich.: William B. Eerdmans Publishing Co., 1981); *Demonism: How to Win Against the Devil,* by Charles R. Swindoll (Portland, Oreg.: Multnomah Press, 1981); and *Biblical Demonology,* by Merrill F. Unger (Wheaton, Ill.: Scripture Press, 1952).

*Living Insights*

**Study One** ▬▬▬▬▬▬▬▬▬▬▬▬▬▬▬▬▬▬▬▬▬▬▬▬▬

Demonic involvement. Talk about a subject that will arouse curiosity! This is a difficult issue, given to many viewpoints. Wise Bible students need to study this topic for themselves to come to their own conclusions.

• With 1 Corinthians 10 as your starting point, begin exploring the Scriptures to help make up your mind about demon involvement in the life of the believer. Use the following questions as a springboard.

1. Can demons affect Christians? If so, how? If not, why not?
2. Is there a difference between "demon oppression" and "demon possession"?
3. What kind of effect does occult involvement have in the life of a Christian?
4. How would you describe Satan's strategy in your life?

 *Living Insights*

**Study Two** ▬▬▬▬▬▬▬▬▬▬▬▬▬▬▬▬▬▬▬▬▬▬▬▬▬

A discussion of demonic activity must lead to the issue of resistance. How do we fight the devil? Did the Lord leave us defenseless against the forces of evil? Let's use our time to create a strategy for victory over demonic involvement in our lives.

• In the space below write your own strategy for defeating Satan and his host of demons. Be sure to base it on Scripture.

**My Strategy for Victory over Satan's Attacks**

_____

_____

_____

_____

_____

_____

_____

_____

_____

# Our Ultimate Objective
*1 Corinthians 10:23–11:1*

In one of his most significant works, *One Day in the Life of Ivan Denisovich,* Alexander Solzhenitsyn presents an unadorned and disturbing picture of life in a Siberian concentration camp.

The protagonist, Ivan Denisovich, has been unjustly sentenced to ten years of grueling labor. But Solzhenitsyn chooses not to unfold for us the long years that stretched before the prisoner but to narrow our focus, letting us experience with Ivan the regime of just one day—"from the first clang of the rail to the last clang of the rail."[1]

Many of the statements Solzhenitsyn makes in *One Day in the Life* are profoundly relevant to our society. They deal with large-scale issues—political loyalty, human dignity, faith. These topics are laced throughout the book, treated on almost every page.

But amid these skyscraper themes, the author has strewn a few single-story ones that get obscured in the shadows and rarely catch the critics' eyes.

One such theme is the purpose our lives can have if we live with a clear, ultimate objective set before us.

Ivan Denisovich—although hungry and chilled to the bone in Siberia's black, sub-zero winter—had a job to do, a reason to face the morning. His task was to build a wall from brick and mortar. All day. And he took simple pride in just knowing he had made it through another day and built a fine wall.

Just as Ivan Denisovich built his wall with barrows of brick and buckets of mortar, so Paul, as "a wise master builder" lays brick upon brick to strengthen believers' lives (1 Cor. 3:10). In 10:23–11:1 of the same book, he concludes the issue of eating sacrificial meat by laying a few guidelines and cementing them in some solid principles that set up our ultimate reason for living.

## I. Timely Guidelines for Corinthians

Before getting up to our elbows in the mortar of this lesson, let's refresh our memories about the questions on the Corinthians' minds: As believers, should we eat sacrificial, idolatrous meat? Can meat be contaminated by its association? These issues can be broken into three parts. We've already dealt with the first one—dining in an idol's temple. Here we will listen to Paul's words on the other two issues.

---

1. Alexander Solzhenitsyn, *One Day in the Life of Ivan Denisovich* (New York, N.Y.: E. P. Dutton and Co., 1963), p. 158.

**A. In the meat market.** As the foundation for his guidelines, Paul lays the first two bricks in verse 25:

> Eat anything that is sold in the meat market, without asking questions for conscience' sake.

First, he puts no restrictions on their shopping list. There is nothing wrong with the meat itself, as there is no substance to an idol (see 8:4). But with this liberty comes the advice not to be unduly introspective about it. Paul's message is "There's no problem with doing it. So if you're going to do it, don't make an issue out of nothing. Just enjoy it."

---
**A Word to the Intense**

It's possible to be overscrupulous about our lives . . . to be so self-analytical, so intense, so edge-of-the-chairish that we cannot enjoy anything within the framework of the Christian life for fear of what someone may think or say.

Sound like you? If so, maybe you need to sit back in your spiritual chair for awhile—relax about what others might be thinking about you and start taking seriously what's important to God (see Eph. 5:1, Phil. 2:3–8).[2]

---

**B. At the dinner party.** Next, Paul moves from the private issue of the meat market to the more public issue of the dinner party. Involving other people—and therefore other consciences—makes this issue more complicated. So Paul makes his principle out of heavier brick.

> If one of the unbelievers invites you, and you wish to go, eat anything that is set before you, without asking questions for conscience' sake. But if anyone should say to you, "This is meat sacrificed to idols," do not eat it, for the sake of the one who informed you, and for conscience' sake. (1 Cor. 10:27–28)

As with the meat market issue, Paul tells the dinner party guests that they are free to go and eat whatever is served, even if unbelievers are there.[3] But the rub comes when someone makes an issue out of the meat. In those situations, Paul tells them to bridle their liberty—for the sake of others.

---

2. One of the first steps toward emotional or mental illness is creating problems out of nothing—being too intense about life, taking it all too seriously. For an excellent discussion of this topic, see *Why Christians Crack Up: The Causes of and Remedies for Nervous Trouble in Christians,* by Marion H. Nelson (Chicago, Ill.: Moody Press, 1960).

3. Some believers will tell us never to associate with the unsaved. But if we follow Jesus' example, we will rub social shoulders with them often, faithfully showing them God's love (see John 4:7–42; Matt. 9:10–12, 18:11; Luke 15:1–2).

1. **A first-century illustration.** Imagine this. You're an active member of the church at Corinth—very involved and very respected. You've been invited to a patio party by Rufus and Julia, a non-Christian couple who own the R & J Chariot Shop on Coliseum Way. They have also invited a young man named Erastus who, unknown to them, has recently come to know the Lord and become a member of the church you attend. You all sit down, and the meal is served. Enjoying your Caesar salad, you look across the table and see a familiar face—Erastus, the new believer who has begun attending your Sunday school class. You smile and chat a little; then your attention is diverted by a delicious-smelling entrée: sirloin steak, delicately seasoned and cooked to perfection. Just as you're reaching for your fork, Erastus leans over to you and whispers, "I just heard the cooks talking about how they were glad so much meat was left over from the sacrifice. You know, that bothers me, because I was involved in idol worship for a long time. I just don't feel right about eating this meat." What do you do? Mustering all the resistance you have, you leave the meat on your plate and politely say, "Please pass the grapes . . . rolls . . . broccoli." You skip the meat—*because an issue was made.*

2. **A twentieth-century illustration.** Picture yourself at a late-night gathering with another believer. You get some punch, and your friend says to you, "Hey . . . smells like there's something more in here than just juice. I used to be an alcoholic—this is a real struggle for me." At that point, you should set your glass down and ask for a 7-UP. Why? Because an issue was made. And not offending others is more important than exercising your own liberty. As Paul explains:

   > Give no offense[4] either to Jews or to Greeks or to the church of God; just as I also please all men in all things, not seeking my own profit, but the profit of the many, that they may be saved. (vv. 32–33)

## II. Timeless Principles for All Christians

If you revel in your liberty, these guidelines will make you cringe. They'll leave you screaming "Legalism!!" But if you'll notice how Paul sets these bricks of truth in steel-and-mortar principles, you'll see that at the end of his argument, like Ivan Denisovich at the end of his day, Paul has built a strong, sturdy wall of truth.

---

4. This phrase can be translated " 'Do not cause anyone to stumble.' " See *Word Meanings in the New Testament,* by Ralph Earle (Grand Rapids, Mich.: Baker Book House, 1986), p. 233. For biblical references about causing a fellow believer to stumble, see Luke 17:2 and 1 Corinthians 8:12–13.

**A. The profit principle.** Liberty is not to be exercised at others' expense, but for their profit.

> All things are lawful, but not all things are profitable. All things are lawful, but not all things edify. (v. 23; see also Rom. 14:19–20)

If your liberty brings someone else into bondage, it's not really liberty at all. Like a mother with small children who sleeps in till noon, creating disaster in the home, so believers who abuse their liberty leave the weaker brother in God's family offended and hurt, spiritually bruised.

---
**Building Up**

Each of us is like a wheelbarrow full of loose bricks—dependent on the skillful hands of others to build us up, to help us see the clear-cut truth of God's love.

What kind of craftsmanship have you been using in others' lives lately? Are you building others up ... filling in the cracks ... troweling away the loose grit? Or, because of your careless touch—an abused liberty—is another believer lying still in the wheelbarrow, a pile of chipped, broken bricks?

---

**B. The people principle.** With this principle, Paul slaps another layer of mortar onto his guidelines.

> Let no one seek his own good, but that of his neighbor.... Just as I also please all men in all things, not seeking my own profit, but the profit of the many, that they may be saved. (1 Cor. 10:24, 33)

In this context, Paul is talking about looking out for the well-being of others (see Phil. 2:3–4), not currying their favor so that they might think well of you (see Gal. 1:10). His concern is that we do what's *best* for others.

**C. The planet principle.** Our enjoyment of God's earth should be as infinite as His creation. We ought to be having a ball!

> For the earth is the Lord's, and all it contains. (1 Cor. 10:26)

In many people's minds, God is the grumpy ogre in the sky who sits near the edge of heaven with a big, ugly club and whomps you every time you start having any fun. But this isn't the God pictured in 1 Timothy 6:17. There we see a God "who richly supplies us with all things to enjoy" (see also 4:4). Paul doesn't mean to wet-blanket our enjoyment of life, but he does want us to treat tenderly the consciences of our weaker brothers.

**D. The primary principle.** With the mortar of this last principle, Paul finishes his argument. He wipes off his trowel and leaves standing before us our ultimate objective—the plumb line of truth.

> Whether, then, you eat or drink or whatever you do, *do all to the glory of God.* (1 Cor. 10:31, emphasis added)

---

### One Day in Your Life

For Ivan Denisovich, it was as simple as having a wall to build. That's what gave his life meaning—what gave him the strength to endure the hunger pangs, the sickness, the cruelty, the injustice he experienced each day.

Most of us don't have to live under such dire conditions. But we still have to have a reason to get up in the morning.

What objective do you live by? Is your primary concern bringing glory to God? Or are you clinging so tightly to your freedom in the Lord that you're tearing down your brothers and bringing shame to His name?

At the end of *One Day in the Life,* a fellow prisoner, Alyosha, asks Ivan:

> "Why do you want freedom? In freedom your last grain of faith will be choked with weeds. You should rejoice that you're in prison. Here you have time to think about your soul. As the Apostle Paul wrote: 'Why all these tears? Why are you trying to weaken my resolution? For my part I am ready not merely to be bound but even to die for the name of the Lord Jesus.'"[5]

---

 *Living Insights*

**Study One** ▰▰▰▰▰▰▰▰▰▰▰▰▰▰▰▰▰▰▰▰▰▰▰▰▰

The last few lessons have all dealt with the issue of meat offered to idols. Though not at the top of today's stress list, this ancient issue does offer some guidelines that apply to present-day struggles. Before we glean these principles, let's take time to further understand the text.

- Earlier in this study guide we walked through the process of paraphrasing. Let's return to that concept with 1 Corinthians 10:23–11:1.

---

5. Solzhenitsyn, *One Day in the Life,* p. 155.

Get behind the words to the level of feelings and beyond the syntax to discover the meanings. Don't be in a hurry with this exercise—it's an important one.

**1 Corinthians 10:23–11:1**

_____

_____

_____

_____

_____

_____

_____

_____

_____

_____

_____

_____

_____

 *Living Insights*

**Study Two** ▬▬▬▬▬▬▬▬▬▬▬▬▬▬▬▬▬▬▬▬▬▬▬

You cannot employ God's principles if you don't know Him! It would be well worth our time to give attention to God Himself. We can do this by talking to Him through prayer.

• We often get so wrapped up in the application of principles—which in itself is not bad—that we tend to overlook the God of those principles. Use this time to talk with God. Thank Him for His involvement in your life. Bring your needs before Him. Speak with Him about His will for you, and get to know Him better. Make this a time of worship, praise, and thanks.

# Pros and Cons of Hair and Hats

*1 Corinthians 11:2–16*

Picture yourself on a ship during World War II, drifting into a harbor's quiet mouth.

Although the waters are calm, the skies clear, you stop and wait for the harbor pilot to take the ship's wheel and weave you through the pathless waters leading to the dock.

At first this seems unnecessary, since the dock is clearly visible just a ways ahead. But as you look over the ship's railing into the glassy water, you begin to understand why.

Strategically hidden beneath the water's wavy surface are highly charged mines that will explode if nudged by a ship's hull. And only the harbor pilot knows where they are. So he steers you through the waters, discreetly dodging the lurking mines.

Like the waters of this harbor, the waters of 1 Corinthians 11 are not difficult, but they *are* delicate. They are charged with explosive issues that have brought disaster to many churches.

The first question raised by the Corinthians in this passage is whether or not women should wear coverings on their heads in worship. Because this was a loaded issue, Paul steers them gently through it to the dock of truth.

## I. The Doctrinal Foundation

Before plunging into his argument, Paul praises the Corinthians for following the teaching he had given while living with them.

> Now I praise you because you remember me in everything, and hold firmly to the traditions, just as I delivered them to you. (1 Cor. 11:2)

But apparently, there were those who drifted from his instruction, creating divisions and cliques in the body (see v. 18). So Paul straightens their course, taking them back to the doctrinal foundation . . . back to the basics.

**A. God's hierarchy.** He starts with a reminder about God's chain of command in the family:

> But I want you to understand that Christ is the head of every man, and the man is the head of a woman, and God is the head of Christ. (v. 3)

From the first link to the last, the chain of command starts with God the Father and moves to God the Son, man, and finally, woman. This hierarchy isn't to establish superiority or inferiority, but to help maintain order in the family.[1]

**B. Man's headship.** If the skeleton of God's truth is verse 3, the flesh, blood, and skin begin in verse 4:

> Every man who has something on his head while praying or prophesying, disgraces[2] his head.

Why? Because a covering on the head is a symbol of submission, and it is a disgrace for the head of the home to wear the marks of submission. Like a battleship that waves a white flag after it has sunk its enemy, so for a man to cover his head is absurd—the symbol, unfitting.

**C. Woman's worship.** With God's chain of command in mind, however, it was fitting for women to cover their heads. This was to remind them that men were in authority and encourage them to have an attitude of submission. About those who refused to be veiled, Paul says:

> But every woman who has her head uncovered while praying or prophesying, disgraces her head; for she is one and the same with her whose head is shaved. For if a woman does not cover her head, let her also have her hair cut off; but if it is disgraceful for a woman to have her hair cut off or her head shaved, let her cover her head. (vv. 5–6)

Paul likens unveiled women to those with shaved heads, to those who have declared their independence from man's authority. So, with sarcasm, he encourages women with this attitude to go all out and cut off their hair and display—physically—the attitude in their hearts.

---
**Wearing Attitudes**

If this custom were practiced in your church, do you think you'd find women with no coverings . . . men wearing veils?

What about you? Men, have you embraced your God-given role of authority in the family? And women, is there a spiritual veil of submission covering your head?

---

1. Being a God of order, not confusion, He has established His pattern in three other areas. There is a personal order, where believers go directly to God in prayer (see Heb. 4:14–16, 7:25). There is also a divine order in church authority; Hebrews 13:7 tells us that preachers and teachers of the Word are to be imitated. Finally, there's a chain of command in the realm of government, which says to submit until the government clashes with God's laws (see Rom. 13:1–7, 1 Pet. 2:13–14).

2. The word *disgrace* is no bland term. It's a word that communicates something that is shockingly evil; in the New Testament it is most often used to refer to sins of sensuality, especially the confusion of sex roles (compare Rom. 1:26–27).

## II. The Biblical Facts

Paul began his argument with generalities, but now he moves in with specifics. In verses 7–10, he presents the biblical facts, careful still not to nudge any of the explosives that mine this volatile issue.

**A. The order of creation.** Reminding them of God's original intent in creating man and woman, Paul beefs up his case:

> For a man ought not to have his head covered, since
> he is the image and glory of God; but the woman is
> the glory of man. (v. 7)

A man, created to be the glory of God, is under moral obligation not to have his head covered. But a woman is to be the glory of the man. God reveals His plan in Genesis 2:18.

> Then the Lord God said, "It is not good for the man
> to be alone; I will make him a helper[3] suitable for
> him."

*Helper* is the first descriptive term in the Bible used for a woman. It doesn't come from the Hebrew word for *doormat*—it's not a term of inferiority but of assistance. And *suitable* means "counterpart, one who completes what is missing in man." God made woman for the man, not the other way around. Man was created first, and woman was derived from him to assist and complete him—to be his glory (1 Cor. 11:8–9).

**B. The realm of angels.** With verse 10, Paul nearly bumps into an underwater mine, charged and dangerous.

> Therefore the woman ought to have a symbol of
> authority on her head, because of the angels.

In this verse, Paul appears to contradict everything he has been saying. He's been referring to the head covering as a symbol of submission, but now he calls it "a symbol of authority." What does he mean? His point is that women are morally obligated to accept the male authority God has provided for them.[4] The focus is on a woman's attitude toward man's authority—her acceptance of it—not the symbol she wears to express her submission. And because the angels are watching, it's an attitude

---

3. "This word is generally used to designate divine aid, particularly in Psalms [compare Ps. 121:1–2] where it includes both material and spiritual assistance." From *Theological Wordbook of the Old Testament,* vol. 2, ed. R. Laird Harris (Chicago, Ill.: Moody Press, 1980), p. 661.

4. Supporting this interpretation is the presence of the preposition *on* in this verse. Every time Paul refers to the wearing of a veil in this passage, he uses the word meaning "down"—as a hat is worn down on the head. Because the word changes in verse 10 to *epi,* meaning "upon" the head, we can conclude that Paul isn't talking about the covering here, but about an attitude toward the authority God has placed *upon* the woman.

that should be upheld (see also 4:9, Eph. 3:10, 1 Tim. 5:21, and Heb. 13:2).[5]

> ┌─ *Settling for Appearances* ─────────────────────
> For God, the heart has always been more important than the appearance. Remember His words to Samuel when he went to anoint a man to replace Saul as king:
>
> "Do not look at his appearance or at the height
> of his stature . . . for God sees not as man sees,
> for man looks at the outward appearance, but
> the Lord looks at the heart." (1 Sam. 16:7)
>
> Sure, we can wear a covering. But is it a sign of true submission, or simply a veil to mask our rebellion?
>
> Just remember, God can see right through, straight to the heart (see Ps. 139:1–4).

## III. The Needed Balance

So far, Paul has impressed us with the necessity for women to accept being under man's authority. To avoid presenting only one side of the issue, the diplomatic Paul gives us a look at the flip side.

**A. The evidence from birth.** Showing the equality and mutual dependence of man and woman, Paul tells us:

> However, in the Lord, neither is woman independent of man, nor is man independent of woman. For as the woman originates from the man, so also the man has his birth through the woman; and all things originate from God. (1 Cor. 11:11–12)

The woman is an essential, invaluable part of God's plan. In His plan, men and women are equal—possessing different roles, but equal.

**B. The evidence from nature.** Approaching yet another mined harbor, Paul begins his last argument:

> Judge for yourselves: is it proper for a woman to pray to God with head uncovered? Does not even nature itself teach you that if a man has long hair, it is a dishonor to him, but if a woman has long hair, it is a glory to her? (vv. 13–15a)

5. In mentioning the angels here, it looks like Paul has gone off on a tangent. But one commentator explains the relation of the angels to the previous verses by stating "that the angels are here mentioned because they were God's agents in the work of creation, of which mention was made [in verses 8 and 9] and therefore sure to be particularly offended by a mode of acting opposed to the normal relation established in the beginning between man and woman." From *Commentary on First Corinthians,* by Frederic Louis Godet (1889; reprint, Grand Rapids, Mich.: Kregel Publications, 1977), p. 551.

*Nature* refers to an inner sense of our distinction, a built-in sense of our sex. There's something about obscuring the differences between the sexes that should naturally offend us. And that inner nature has to be calloused, altered through a hardening of the spirit, before we welcome a change in that distinction.

## IV. Some Practical Advice

Although this issue isn't difficult in Paul's mind, he reminds the Corinthians that it is a delicate one, liable to cause some explosions. But in the same breath, he lets them know how important it is and that he isn't about to budge on it (v. 16). The truths of this issue are timeless, they speak directly to us, even in a day when the physical symbol of hair and hats has lost much of its significance.

**A. Matters of fashion and style are personal.** Search the whole Bible and you still won't find a scissor length for haircuts. Just remember that no matter what style you adopt, it's your heart, not your appearance, that matters.

**B. Your style should support your sexual identity, not obscure it.** When it comes to fashion, do you listen to the sense of masculinity or femininity within you? Or do you ignore it, buying into today's androgynous thinking?

**C. We should willingly adapt our style to glorify God.** This is where the passage really gets delicate . . . where the rub is. Is your style consistent with the image God wants for you—His image? Is it clean and modest? Does it keep your role distinct? If not, are you willing to change it? Because the really important thing is to display God's glory. And that's never out of style!

 *Living Insights*

**Study One** ■■■■■■■■■

In many respects, the issue of women wearing hats to church is a lot like eating meat offered to idols—it's a topical issue that reflects a timeless principle. Let's look at what the timeless Word of God has to say about women.

- What does the Bible say about women, their roles, their responsibilities, their similarities and differences with men? Find a Bible concordance and look up the headings "woman" and "women." Pick out key references and record your observations in the chart on the following page.

| A Biblical View of Women | |
|---|---|
| References | Observations |
|  |  |
|  |  |
|  |  |
|  |  |
|  |  |
|  |  |
|  |  |
|  |  |
|  |  |
|  |  |
|  |  |

 *Living Insights*

**Study Two**

There's no doubt that the Bible exalts women. But do Christians? Let's set a trend and start exalting the women in our lives.

- Do something special for a woman you know. Surprise her with something she especially enjoys. You could send her a bouquet of flowers or take her to her favorite restaurant or send her a card expressing your appreciation for her. Remember, do something that exalts her.

# Eucharist Etiquette Then and Now

*1 Corinthians 11:17–34*

Family reunions are almost a thing of the past. Many people would be hard-pressed even to name their relatives and the cities they live in, much less tell the tales of the last time they spent together. Families just don't gather like they used to. And many wouldn't make it through a reunion anyway, because strife, like a thistly vine, would strangle from the gathering every trace of relaxation and joy.

But there was a time when family reunions were as regular as birds heading south for the winter. Members of the family would flock to the reunion site and settle in for a time of laughing, eating, and rekindling closeness.

In the same way that our natural families need to reunite to strengthen their bonds, so we in the family of God need times of sharing and feasting—times to tighten our family ties.

The night before His crucifixion, Jesus instituted a family reunion—the Lord's Supper (Matt. 26:26–30). In this memorial service, believers may participate together in the most meaningful, the most intimate form of worship.

## I. The Church's Practice

The love feast, or *agapē* feast, was like a modern-day potluck. Members of a church family would gather and bring whatever food or drink they could afford. They were encouraged to share it all, regardless of how rich or poor they were. After the feast, the most symbolic part of the meal was served—the *Eucharist.*[1] It included the breaking and eating of bread to commemorate Jesus' crucified body and drinking from a cup of wine in remembrance of the blood He shed for our sins. After the meal, the believers would linger to share and sing and enjoy a time where all barriers were down and all bonds strengthened.

## II. The Corinthians' Situation

Like everything else man has touched, he ruined even the Lord's Supper. In 1 Corinthians 11:17–34, we see that the Corinthians had turned what was intended to be a feast of love and remembrance into a gluttonous orgy of pride and selfishness. Small wonder Paul refused to praise them!

**A. Paul's introductory comments.** When it comes to his rebuke on this issue, Paul doesn't mince words.

---

1. *Eucharist* means "thanksgiving," telling us something of the purpose for partaking in the bread and the cup.

> But in giving this instruction, I do not praise you,
> because you come together not for the better but for
> the worse. (v. 17)

In verse 2 of this chapter, Paul had something to praise them about. But now the reason for praising them has disappeared. Because they had so perverted the Lord's Supper, he wishes they had never observed it at all.

**B. Paul's condemnation.** This severe beginning sets Paul's tone for the rest of the chapter, as he continues to blast the Corinthians:

> For, in the first place, when you come together as a
> church, I hear that divisions exist among you; and in
> part, I believe it. For there must also be factions
> among you, in order that those who are approved
> may have become evident among you. Therefore
> when you meet together, it is not to eat the Lord's
> Supper. (vv. 18–20)

Though the Corinthians were supposed to be gathered to celebrate their unity in Christ, they huddled instead into exclusive little groups—barriered, proud, selfish.

> For in your eating each one takes his own supper
> first; and one is hungry and another is drunk. What!
> Do you not have houses in which to eat and drink?
> Or do you despise the church of God, and shame
> those who have nothing? What shall I say to you?
> Shall I praise you? In this I will not praise you.
> (vv. 21–22)

Like a group of whining two-year-olds, they clung to what they could call "Mine!" Drunken and gorged on their own food and drink, they hadn't yet learned to share. So, because of their selfishness, Paul shakes in their faces the scathing finger of condemnation.

---

*Ritual or Reality?*

In the first century, the Church had eased the social problems that baffled Rome and still baffle the world. They had lifted women to their rightful place, restored the dignity of labor, abolished begging, and softened the sting of slavery.

The secret of their revolution was that the selfishness of race and class was set aside. They freed themselves from prejudice. All distinctions, all barriers were to be ignored (see Gal. 3:28).

No sacrament expressed this more vividly than the Lord's Supper. It provided the Church with a visible symbol of their unity and equality in Christ—in His broken body, and in the blood He shed for us all.

We have seen that in their celebration of the Lord's Supper, the Corinthians completely ruined this harmonious picture. What about you and your church? Do you uphold the unique value of every member? Or do you judge members according to race, social class, or sex? If Paul were writing a letter to your church on this issue, would he refuse to praise you too?

Let's learn from the Corinthians' mistakes. Let's not take something as holy as communion and, by our prejudices, make it a travesty.

## III. Jesus' Instruction

Like any good teacher, Paul doesn't leave the Corinthians wallowing in what they've done *wrong,* but follows his condemning speech with instruction for the *right* way to celebrate the Eucharist—taken from the very words of Jesus.

**A. The meal's elements.** This instruction was nothing new to the Corinthians. As Paul says:

> For I received from the Lord that which I also delivered to you. (1 Cor. 11:23a)

But, ears filled with their own prideful voices, they hadn't listened. So he tells them again.

> The Lord Jesus in the night in which He was betrayed took bread; and when He had given thanks, He broke it, and said, "This is My body, which is for you; do this in remembrance of Me." (vv. 23b–24)

That black night when Judas would betray Him, Jesus gathered His disciples together to celebrate the Passover meal. But no paschal lamb was present at this celebration. Instead, Jesus—the Lamb of God—stood before them and spoke of His death, the ultimate sacrifice. Methodically, He took the bread . . . gave thanks for it . . . broke it . . . and distributed it. Then He took a goblet of wine and said:

> "This cup is the new covenant[2] in My blood; do this, as often as you drink it, in remembrance of Me." (v. 25b)

Paul brings this point home, saying, "For as often as you eat this bread and drink the cup, you proclaim the Lord's death until He comes" (v. 26).

2. *Covenant* means "a promise or pact between two parties in which there is a mutual agreement." The Old Covenant was based on Moses' Law. And the New Covenant is based on Jesus' blood—His sacrifice for us. While those under the Law are condemned, those covered by the blood of the New Covenant are free from all condemnation (see Rom. 8:1).

**B. The meal's purpose.** Jesus makes the purpose clear in repeating the phrase "in remembrance of Me." Communion is a time for the family of God to reunite around His Table and commemorate His death. There's nothing sacred about the bread and wine themselves. They are significant only because they physically represent His body and blood.[3] Whether you use bread and wine or crackers and grape juice, the meal's essentials are the same—family, thanksgiving, sharing, and Christ. Nothing else matters.

---

### God of Show, Not Tell

Educators tell us that the more senses we use in the process of learning, the more likely we are to retain and apply our knowledge.

Looking back at biblical history, it seems that the Lord would agree.

When He told Noah He would never flood the earth again, He sealed His promise with a physical sign—a rainbow (Gen. 9:11–13).

When He told man and wife to cleave to each other, to become one flesh, He gave them sex—a physical expression of their intimacy and oneness.

And when telling us to remember His death, He asks us to "*do this,*" to taste and touch His death—so that we would really remember.[4]

---

## IV. Paul's Application

After presenting the ideal for this family reunion, Paul returns to the wreck the Corinthians had made of it.

**A. The offense.** One of the house rules about the Lord's Supper was that you were to dress for the occasion, casting off the rags of pride, selfishness, gluttony, and drunkenness. Paul spells out the seriousness of disobedience, saying,

---

3. A view known as *transubstantiation* conveys the idea that the bread actually becomes Jesus' body; and the cup, His blood. For some background information on this view, see: *Worship in the Early Church*, by Ralph P. Martin (1964; reprint, Grand Rapids, Mich.: William B. Eerdmans Publishing Co., 1978), chaps. 10–11; *The Church in God's Program*, by Robert L. Saucy (Chicago, Ill.: Moody Press, 1972), pp. 213–17.

4. Jesus' phrase " 'in remembrance of me' . . . is no bare historical reflection upon the Cross, but a recalling of the crucified and living Christ in such a way that He is personally present in all the fulness and reality of His saving power, and is appropriated by the believers' faith." Martin, *Worship in the Early Church*, p. 126.

Therefore whoever eats the bread or drinks the cup of the Lord in an unworthy manner,[5] shall be guilty of the body and the blood of the Lord. (1 Cor. 11:27)

**B. The punishment.** Those who come to the Lord's Table with unclean hearts are sure to be disciplined:

For he who eats and drinks, eats and drinks judgment to himself, if he does not judge the body rightly. For this reason many among you are weak and sick, and a number sleep.... But when we are judged, we are disciplined by the Lord in order that we may not be condemned along with the world. (vv. 29, 30, 32)

This discipline isn't purely punitive, but is fatherly, bringing offenders to repentance so they won't be judged (see Heb. 12:5–7).

**C. The solution.** Mingled in with Paul's negative words is some advice on how to avoid displeasing our heavenly Father.

But let a man examine himself, and so let him eat of the bread and drink of the cup.... If we judged ourselves rightly, we should not be judged. (vv. 28, 31)

Before taking communion, we must plead with the Lord as David did:

Search me, O God, and know my heart;
Try me and know my anxious thoughts;
And see if there be any hurtful way in me,
And lead me in the everlasting way. (Ps. 139:23–24)

---

*Table Manners*

When celebrating the Lord's Supper, how are your table manners? Do you eat with unwashed hands? Do you share the meal grudgingly?

Remember what this family reunion represents. Enjoy it with wholehearted thanksgiving ... and reverence.

---

5. The phrase "in an unworthy manner" has been explained in a host of ways: with a bad conscience and without repentance; with contempt for the poor; without faith in the words *given for you;* without self-examination. "The explanation to which the context naturally leads is this: Without the grateful memory of Christ's sufferings, a memory which necessarily implies the breaking of the will with sin." From *Commentary on First Corinthians,* by Frederic Louis Godet (1889; reprint, Grand Rapids, Mich.: Kregel Publications, 1977), pp. 591–92.

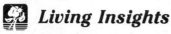 *Living Insights*

Believe it or not, you are now two-thirds of the way through 1 Corinthians! Now we will spend some time reviewing what we've learned from this series.

● Listed below are the titles of the twelve lessons we have just finished studying. Looking back over your Bible and study guide, choose from each lesson one truth that's been significant to you. Don't worry about the applications you've made—we'll cover those in Study Two.

### Practical Helps for a Hurting Church

My Body and Me _____

_____

_____

Single or Married—Which Is Better? _____

_____

_____

God's Answer to the Unhappy Marriage _____

_____

_____

Biblical Advice on Staying Single _____

_____

_____

Love, Liberty, and the Meat Problem _____

_____

_____

Bottom of the Ninth, Score's Tied, You're Up _____

_____

_____

*Continued on next page*

In the Arena _____

_____

_____

Please Follow the Instructions . . . or Else! _____

_____

_____

Idol Altars and Demon Activity Today _____

_____

_____

Our Ultimate Objective _____

_____

_____

Pros and Cons of Hair and Hats _____

_____

_____

Eucharist Etiquette Then and Now _____

_____

_____

 *Living Insights*

**Study Two** ▬▬▬▬▬▬▬▬▬▬▬▬▬▬▬▬▬▬▬▬▬▬▬▬▬▬▬▬▬▬

It is always our hope that you'll apply what you've learned in these studies. Did your life change as a result of these lessons? Reviewing what you've learned will encourage you in your personal growth.

- The following list is just like the one in the previous study, but this time look at ways you've applied what you've learned. Choose just one application from each lesson and jot it down next to the corresponding title.

# Practical Helps for a Hurting Church

My Body and Me _____

_____

_____

Single or Married—Which Is Better? _____

_____

_____

God's Answer to the Unhappy Marriage _____

_____

_____

Biblical Advice on Staying Single _____

_____

_____

Love, Liberty, and the Meat Problem _____

_____

_____

Bottom of the Ninth, Score's Tied, You're Up _____

_____

_____

In the Arena _____

_____

_____

Please Follow the Instructions . . . or Else! _____

_____

_____

*Continued on next page*

Idol Altars and Demon Activity Today _____

_____

_____

Our Ultimate Objective _____

_____

_____

Pros and Cons of Hair and Hats _____

_____

_____

Eucharist Etiquette Then and Now _____

_____

_____

# Books for Probing Further

When it came to sin, the Corinthians knew it all: immorality . . . idolatry . . . licentiousness . . . *pride*.

After hearing Paul discuss issue after issue and give rebuke after rebuke, you probably had one of two responses. You may have wanted to poke a contemptuous finger at the Corinthians' numb-heartedness—at their spiritual ignorance. Or, seeing a little of *your* image in the Corinthian mirror, you may have been moved to change.

In a parable, Jesus personifies both responses:

> "Two men went up into the temple to pray, one a Pharisee, and the other a tax-gatherer. The Pharisee stood and was praying thus to himself, 'God, I thank Thee that I am not like other people: swindlers, unjust, adulterers, or even like this tax-gatherer. I fast twice a week; I pay tithes of all that I get.' But the tax-gatherer, standing some distance away, was even unwilling to lift up his eyes to heaven, but was beating his breast, saying, 'God, be merciful to me, the sinner!' I tell you, this man went down to his house justified rather than the other; for everyone who exalts himself shall be humbled, but he who humbles himself shall be exalted." (Luke 18:10–14)

Sadly, our pharisee-eyes, full of logs, are too often focused on the specks in everyone else's lives (see Matt. 7:3–5). So, before thanking God that you're *not* like the Corinthians, I urge you to search your heart to find the ways you *are*. Remember, the real issues weren't the wearing of hats or the eating of meat offered to idols. The crux of their problems was a lack of love due to pride—a sin that ensnares us all.

It's my hope that the resources we've listed will give you practical help in the issues you face . . . and that you'll have the courage, like the tax-gatherer, to see yourself realistically, admit your sin humbly, and decide wholeheartedly to obey the Lord.

Adams, Jay E. *Marriage, Divorce, and Remarriage*. Phillipsburg, N.J.: Presbyterian and Reformed Publishing Co., 1980. With the divorce rate climbing even in Christian circles, the questions surrounding marriage, divorce, and remarriage demand straight answers. In this clear, practical discussion, Adams offers biblical answers to these sensitive issues.

Hocking, David. *Marrying Again: A Guide for Christians*. Old Tappan, N.J.: Fleming H. Revell Co., 1983. Hocking not only unties the knotty issues surrounding the ethics of remarriage but also deals with the everyday matters unique to those who have remarried.

Kehl, D. G. *Control Yourself! Practicing the Art of Self-Discipline.* Grand Rapids, Mich.: Zondervan Publishing House, 1982. Like the Corinthians, many of us are out of shape because we lack self-control. Our flabbiness may be spiritual, intellectual, emotional, moral, or physical. But don't be discouraged! Kehl provides biblical guidelines that will help us get in shape so we can live healthier, more productive lives.

Lutzer, Erwin W. *Living with Your Passions.* Wheaton, Ill.: Victor Books, 1983. Single or married, young or old, we all have sexual needs that demand fulfillment. In this book, Lutzer sets forth God's standard of sexual purity, explaining how we *can* win the battle against sexual sin while enjoying our sexuality within the protective boundaries of Scripture.

Mason, Mike. *The Mystery of Marriage: As Iron Sharpens Iron.* Portland, Oreg.: Multnomah Press, 1985. Many books on marriage will give you *how to*s, but Mason's work goes a step further and helps you understand the *whys*. His unique insights will rejuvenate your excitement about marriage as they unfold the most mysterious, most intimate relationship any two people can experience.

Schlossberg, Herbert. *Idols for Destruction: Christian Faith and Its Confrontation with American Society.* Nashville, Tenn.: Thomas Nelson Publishers, 1983. We may not bow down to idols as the Corinthians did, but idolatry permeates our society just the same. Illicit sex is pedestaled; pleasure is more important than sacrifice; making a profit overshadows saving a soul; the elderly are discarded and the unborn aborted; false religions and philosophies abound. In this eye-opening book, Schlossberg deals with these issues in one of the most penetrating analyses in print.

Swindoll, Charles R. *Improving Your Serve: The Art of Unselfish Living.* Waco, Tex.: Word Books, 1981. Selfishness . . . the vice we're all born with, that parents spend years trying to spank out of us, that never completely goes away. This book is honest about our continual struggle with selfishness. And, with a gentle nudge of encouragement, it will help you learn the almost lost art of unselfish living.

Unger, Merrill F. *Demons in the World Today.* Wheaton, Ill.: Tyndale House Publishers, 1971. Satan is no myth. He and his angels are active, trying to draw us away from God. We've got to be aware of his strategies if we're to combat him effectively. This book reveals Satan's game plan and explains how we can fight against him, protected by God's armor and fortified by the Holy Spirit.

# Acknowledgments

Insight for Living is grateful for permission to quote from the following sources:

Godet, Frederic Louis. *Commentary on First Corinthians.* 1889. Reprint. Grand Rapids, Mich.: Kregel Publications, 1977.

Mason, Mike. *The Mystery of Marriage: As Iron Sharpens Iron.* Portland, Oreg.: Multnomah Press, 1985.

# Notes

# Notes

# Notes

# Notes

# Insight for Living
## Cassette Tapes
## PRACTICAL HELPS FOR A HURTING CHURCH
### A STUDY OF 1 CORINTHIANS 6:12–11:34

Surrounded by sensuality, inundated with idolatry, the church at Corinth was struggling! Hard issues pressed at them from all sides—singleness or marriage, liberty or license, sexual satiation or purity, idols, demons, submission, communion.

In this central section of Paul's first letter to the Corinthians, he reaches out to help a church he had planted by giving them principles to hang on to—principles inspired by the Holy Spirit—that we can still cling to today.

|  |  |  | U.S. | Canada |
|---|---|---|---|---|
| PHH | CS | Cassette series—includes album cover .... | $34.50 | $43.75 |
|  |  | Individual cassettes—include messages |  |  |
|  |  | A and B ........................ | 5.00 | 6.35 |

*These prices are effective as of February 1988 and are subject to change without notice.*

PHH 1-A: *My Body and Me*—1 Corinthians 6:12–20
   B: *Single or Married—Which Is Better?*—1 Corinthians 7:1–7, 26, 35

PHH 2-A: *God's Answer to the Unhappy Marriage*—1 Corinthians 7:8–16
   B: *Biblical Advice on Staying Single*—1 Corinthians 7:25–35

PHH 3-A: *Love, Liberty, and the Meat Problem*—1 Corinthians 8
   B: *Bottom of the Ninth, Score's Tied, You're Up*—1 Corinthians 9:1–23

PHH 4-A: *In the Arena*—1 Corinthians 9:24–27
   B: *Please Follow the Instructions . . . or Else!*—1 Corinthians 10:1–11

PHH 5-A: *Idol Altars and Demon Activity Today*—1 Corinthians 10:12–22
   B: *Our Ultimate Objective*—1 Corinthians 10:23–11:1

PHH 6-A: *Pros and Cons of Hair and Hats*—1 Corinthians 11:2–16
   B: *Eucharist Etiquette Then and Now*—1 Corinthians 11:17–34

# How to Order by Mail

Ordering is easy and convenient. Simply mark on the order form whether you want the series or individual tapes, including the quantity you desire. Tear out the order form and mail it with your payment to the appropriate address on the bottom of the form. We will process your order as promptly as we can.

**United States orders:** If you wish your order to be shipped first-class for faster delivery, please add 10 percent of the total order amount (not including California sales tax). Otherwise, please allow four to six weeks for delivery by fourth-class mail. We accept personal checks, money orders, Visa, and Master-Card in payment for materials. Unfortunately, we are unable to offer invoicing or COD orders.

**Canadian orders:** Please add 7 percent of your total order for first-class postage and allow approximately four weeks for delivery. For our listeners in British Columbia, a 6 percent sales tax must also be added to the total of all tape orders (not including postage). For further information, please contact our office at (604) 272-5811. We accept personal checks, money orders, Visa, or MasterCard in payment for materials. Unfortunately, we are unable to offer invoicing or COD orders.

**Overseas orders:** If you live outside the United States or Canada, please allow six to ten weeks for delivery by surface mail. If you would like your order sent airmail, the delivery time may be reduced. Whether you choose surface or airmail delivery, postage costs must be added to the amount of purchase and included with your order. Please use the following chart to determine the correct postage. Due to fluctuating currency rates, we can accept only personal checks made payable in U.S. funds, international money orders, Visa, or MasterCard in payment for materials.

| Type of Postage | Cassettes |
| --- | --- |
| Surface | 10% of total order |
| Airmail | 25% of total order |

# For Faster Service, Order by Telephone

To purchase using Visa or MasterCard, you are welcome to use our **toll-free** number between the hours of 8:30 A.M. and 4:00 P.M., Pacific time, Monday through Friday. The number is **1-800-772-8888,** and it may be used anywhere in the United States except California, Hawaii, and Alaska. Telephone orders from these states and overseas are handled through our Sales Department at (714) 870-9161. Canadian residents should call (604) 272-5811. We are unable to accept collect calls.

## Our Guarantee

Our cassettes are guaranteed for ninety days against faulty performance or breakage due to a defect in the tape. For best results, please be sure your tape recorder is in good operating condition and is cleaned regularly.

**Note:** To cover processing and handling, there is a $10 fee for *any* returned check.

# Order Form

PHH CS represents the entire *Practical Helps for a Hurting Church* series, while PHH 1–6 are the individual tapes included in the series.

| Series or Tape | Unit Price U.S. | Unit Price Canada | Quantity | Amount |
|---|---|---|---|---|
| PHH CS | $34.50 | $43.75 | | $ |
| PHH 1 | 5.00 | 6.35 | | |
| PHH 2 | 5.00 | 6.35 | | |
| PHH 3 | 5.00 | 6.35 | | |
| PHH 4 | 5.00 | 6.35 | | |
| PHH 5 | 5.00 | 6.35 | | |
| PHH 6 | 5.00 | 6.35 | | |
| **Subtotal** | | | | |
| **Sales tax** *6% for orders delivered in California or British Columbia* | | | | |
| **Postage** *7% in Canada; overseas residents see "How to Order by Mail"* | | | | |
| **10% optional first-class shipping and handling** *U.S. residents only* | | | | |
| **Gift to Insight for Living** *Tax-deductible in the U.S. and Canada* | | | | |
| **Total amount due** *Please do not send cash.* | | | | $ |

If there is a balance: ☐ apply it as a donation   ☐ please refund

## Form of payment:

☐ Check or money order made payable to Insight for Living

☐ Credit card (circle one):     Visa     MasterCard

Card Number _____ Expiration Date _____

Signature _____
*We cannot process your credit card purchase without your signature.*

Name _____

Address _____

City _____

State/Province_____ Zip/Postal Code _____

Country _____

Telephone (____) _____ Radio Station ___ ___ ___ ___
*If questions arise concerning your order, we may need to contact you.*

## Mail this order form to the Sales Department at one of these addresses:
Insight for Living, Post Office Box 4444, Fullerton, CA 92634
Insight for Living Ministries, Post Office Box 2510, Vancouver, BC, Canada V6B 3W7

# Order Form

PHH CS represents the entire *Practical Helps for a Hurting Church* series, while PHH 1–6 are the individual tapes included in the series.

| Series or Tape | Unit Price U.S. | Canada | Quantity | Amount |
|---|---|---|---|---|
| PHH CS | $34.50 | $43.75 | | $ |
| PHH 1 | 5.00 | 6.35 | | |
| PHH 2 | 5.00 | 6.35 | | |
| PHH 3 | 5.00 | 6.35 | | |
| PHH 4 | 5.00 | 6.35 | | |
| PHH 5 | 5.00 | 6.35 | | |
| PHH 6 | 5.00 | 6.35 | | |
| | | | **Subtotal** | |
| | | | **Sales tax** *6% for orders delivered in California or British Columbia* | |
| | | | **Postage** *7% in Canada; overseas residents see "How to Order by Mail"* | |
| | | | **10% optional first-class shipping and handling** *U.S. residents only* | |
| | | | **Gift to Insight for Living** *Tax-deductible in the U.S. and Canada* | |
| | | | **Total amount due** *Please do not send cash.* | $ |

If there is a balance:  ☐ apply it as a donation  ☐ please refund

**Form of payment:**

☐ Check or money order made payable to Insight for Living

☐ Credit card (circle one):    Visa    MasterCard

    Card Number _____    Expiration Date _____

    Signature _____
    *We cannot process your credit card purchase without your signature.*

Name _____

Address _____

City _____

State/Province _____  Zip/Postal Code _____

Country _____

Telephone (____) _____  Radio Station ___ ___ ___ ___
*If questions arise concerning your order, we may need to contact you.*

**Mail this order form to the Sales Department at one of these addresses:**
Insight for Living, Post Office Box 4444, Fullerton, CA 92634
Insight for Living Ministries, Post Office Box 2510, Vancouver, BC, Canada V6B 3W7

# Order Form

PHH CS represents the entire *Practical Helps for a Hurting Church* series, while PHH 1–6 are the individual tapes included in the series.

| Series or Tape | Unit Price U.S. | Unit Price Canada | Quantity | Amount |
|---|---|---|---|---|
| PHH CS | $34.50 | $43.75 | | $ |
| PHH 1 | 5.00 | 6.35 | | |
| PHH 2 | 5.00 | 6.35 | | |
| PHH 3 | 5.00 | 6.35 | | |
| PHH 4 | 5.00 | 6.35 | | |
| PHH 5 | 5.00 | 6.35 | | |
| PHH 6 | 5.00 | 6.35 | | |
| **Subtotal** | | | | |
| **Sales tax** *6% for orders delivered in California or British Columbia* | | | | |
| **Postage** *7% in Canada; overseas residents see "How to Order by Mail"* | | | | |
| **10% optional first-class shipping and handling** *U.S. residents only* | | | | |
| **Gift to Insight for Living** *Tax-deductible in the U.S. and Canada* | | | | |
| **Total amount due** *Please do not send cash.* | | | | $ |

If there is a balance: ☐ apply it as a donation  ☐ please refund

## Form of payment:

☐ Check or money order made payable to Insight for Living

☐ Credit card (circle one):  Visa  MasterCard

Card Number _____  Expiration Date _____

Signature _____
*We cannot process your credit card purchase without your signature.*

Name _____
Address _____
City _____
State/Province _____  Zip/Postal Code _____
Country _____
Telephone ( ___ ) _____  Radio Station ___ ___ ___ ___
*If questions arise concerning your order, we may need to contact you.*

## Mail this order form to the Sales Department at one of these addresses:
Insight for Living, Post Office Box 4444, Fullerton, CA 92634
Insight for Living Ministries, Post Office Box 2510, Vancouver, BC, Canada V6B 3W7